Karin Calloway's

Quick Cooking II
A Second Serving

Chocolate Chip Pie   page 109

Dedication

This book is dedicated to my darling husband, Bond.

Acknowledgements

To my Heavenly Father – I continue to be amazed at the path you have lain for me, and the wonderful people you have brought into my life.

To Bond, who has been sharing culinary adventures with me for 20 years. Thank you for enjoying and encouraging my professional path!

To Tripp and C.C. – You two always have just the right words of encouragement when I am having a moment of self-doubt! I love you both so much!

To Mom and Dad, who have never for one second stopped being proud parents, and who always give me so much encouragement and love.

To my sister Leslie, for your wisdom beyond your years and for being my best friend. And, to my brother Dave, for your advice and support. I love you both very much.

To Deborah Ashe, who saw my future as a food writer and pushed me to take the leap and follow this path. Thank you so much for your friendship!

To my girlfriends – Renée Link, Martha Long, Robin Merriman and Barbara Mysona – you all keep me sane! Thanks for always listening, supporting and cheering me on in all my endeavors.

To those who put me on the pages of *The Augusta Chronicle* – Elizabeth Adams, Erica Cline, Tharon Giddens, and Jennifer Miller, and to the awesome photographers – Annette M. Drowlette, Jonathan Ernst, Jennifer Fuller, Michael Holahan, Chris Thelen and Andrew Davis Tucker who make it all look so good!

To the Marketing Department of *The Chronicle*: Larry Younginer, for your support of a second cookbook project, Gerry Brown for your beautiful design work, Denise Parrish for your work as my project coordinator, and to my book signing buddies Beth Frits, Stacy Montoya and from my first book, Monica Williams. You all are responsible for making this, and our last cookbook project, possible.

To my "Masters" crowd – Warren and Harriet Stephens, Mark and Laura Doramus, Scott and Dede Ford and Andy Moreau. I love seeing all of you when you return to Augusta each year!

To Fred and Margaret Carl for enjoying my creations during the Masters and for finding a home for me at Viking Range Corporation. And to Jane Crump at Viking for being a wonderful, supportive supervisor!

Last but not least, special thanks to Todd Bennett for your exceptional photography and friendship. Your beautiful photographs never cease to amaze me!

Photographs courtesy of Todd Bennett and Viking Range Corporation, pages 2, 15, 16, 17, 31, 23 (Pazole Blanco), 34, 35, 39,
42 (Warm Asparagus Salad), 60, 61, 62, 70, 87, 88, 98 (Sweet Potato Muffins), 103, 104, 106, 107, 108, 109, 111
Edited by Karin Calloway, Denise H. Parrish and Jennifer Miller

Design by Gerry Brown

Front and back cover photos by John Harpring
Production managed by Denise H. Parrish
Photography by Annette M. Drowlette, Jonathan Ernst, Jennifer Fuller, Michael Holahan, Chris Thelen, Andrew Davis Tucker and Robert Corley
Photo editing by Charles Campbell, Jerel Jones, Rosa Ryan and Sylvia Mead
Photo research by Sean Moores

Cover recipes: Minute Minestrone on page 29, Cheese Calzones on page 99 and Fudge Pound Cake on page 107.

Karin Calloway's

Quick Cooking II
A Second Serving

Introduction

It's amazing how time flies, and that it's been five years since I began sharing quick recipes in the Wednesday "Your Life" section of *The Augusta Chronicle*. My quick cooking philosophy hasn't changed over these years, and I still believe that while the "quick" part of the equation is essential, the finished meals you serve have got to taste great! This cookbook offers delicious recipes, taking the best of the convenience products available at your favorite supermarket, and doctoring them to come up with dishes that far surpass the sum of their parts.

Quick Cooking continues to be essential in my life, as my family and work obligations seem to increase constantly. Between being wife to one hard-working husband, Bond, who puts in many long hours; serving as chauffeur for after-school activities for my children, Tripp and C.C.; serving as President (2003-2004) of the Junior League of Augusta, Georgia, Inc. (a large community service organization); and taking on a new role as cooking correspondent for WJBF NewsChannel 6, my family could be spending a tremendous amount of time and money at the local fast-food drive-thrus.

Fortunately, my profession keeps me in the recipe development and testing mode most of the time, so my "guinea pigs" are well fed. Recipe testing aside, I also use a menu-planning system that any busy family can employ. To help you keep dinner on the table, I've included my menu planning pointers in these pages, along with helpful lists of the items you'll want to keep stocked in your pantry, refrigerator and freezer. A little pre-planning and time in the check-out line will save you money and time in the take-out lane.

For those readers who requested more information with each recipe, I've also included many of the quick tips from my weekly column, along with 22 new recipes that haven't been published in *The Chronicle*. There are a bevy of new hors d'oeuvres, soups and desserts for you to enjoy.

While these five years have flown, this book and the continued popularity of the column would not be possible without my loyal readers. Thank you so much for introducing yourselves to me about town and for your many e-mails and letters. The best part of this job is knowing that my work helps other busy families enjoy a meal together, and I hope to continue to do so for many years to come.

Happy cooking,

Karin Calloway

Pantry & Refrigerator Primers

Quick cooking is next to impossible if you don't have the right ingredients on hand. Items like seasoned diced tomatoes, diced green chilies, reduced-sodium condensed soups, chicken broth and canned legumes help hurried cooks get dinner on the table fast.

To help you solve your "What's for dinner?" dilemma,

I've compiled a list of pantry and refrigerator must-haves. With these ingredients on hand you can prepare practically every recipe in this cookbook! Don't be overwhelmed, however, by the length of this list. Take a look at my menu planning tips which will help you determine what to purchase on a weekly basis.

CANNED GOODS

Must have:
- Diced tomatoes: plain and seasoned with basil, garlic and oregano. (Mexican, chili and lasagna-seasoned diced tomatoes also are good to have on hand.)
- Tomato paste
- Tomato puree or crushed tomatoes
- Tomato sauce
- Spaghetti sauce
- Pizza sauce
- Reduced-sodium broth: chicken and beef
- Reduced-fat and sodium condensed soups: cream of chicken and/or mushroom, tomato and French onion
- Diced green chilies
- Corn niblets and/or Mexicorn
- Canned legumes: black-eyed peas, white beans, black beans, chili beans (with sauce)
- Mandarin orange sections (for salads)
- Pineapple tidbits (for salads, pizza and stirfry)
- Tuna
- Beef gravy (on mashed potatoes or in shepherd's pie)

Occasional use:
- Sun-dried tomatoes (oil-packed or spread)
- Quartered artichoke hearts
- Roasted red bell peppers
- Sliced mushrooms

- Capers
- Chunk and/or white chicken
- Evaporated skim milk
- Minced or baby clams (for dips, pasta and chowder)
- Sliced black olives
- Refried beans (quick side dish, or for nachos, burritos and Mexican meatloaf or pizza)

Special:
- Enchilada sauce
- Alfredo sauce
- Water chestnuts
- Smoked oysters (for quick hors d'oeuvres)

OILS

Must have:
- Nonstick cooking spray
- Olive oil
- Vegetable, canola, corn oil or a blended canola and corn oil

Occasional use:
- Shortening

DRY GOODS

Must have:

- Dried pasta in assorted shapes (long strands including angel hair and spaghetti; short and wide varieties such as ziti and bow-ties; egg noodles and no-boil lasagna noodles)
- Rice: converted white or instant white rice; instant brown rice; packaged rice mixes such as Mexican, chicken, yellow and Uncle Ben's Wild and White Rice mix.
- For baking: sugar, brown sugar, all-purpose flour, baking soda, baking powder, cornstarch and cornmeal
- Baking mix such as Bisquick or Jiffy (for pancakes, waffles, drop biscuits and shortcakes)
- Corn-muffin mix
- Dry breadcrumbs (plain or seasoned)
- Raisins
- Gravy and sauce mixes: Bearnaise or Hollandaise, white and brown sauce mixes
- Mashed potato buds or instant mashed potatoes

Occasional use:

- Dehydrated sun-dried tomatoes (reconstitute in hot water)
- Crumbled bacon pieces
- Graham cracker, chocolate or shortbread pie crusts
- Brownie mix (for a quick dessert or brownie cookies)
- Chocolate chips

Special:

- Dried cranberries

Ham and Cheese Quiche   page 71

SEASONINGS

When it comes to seasonings, I have a pantry packed full of herbs, spices and spice/seasoning blends. Since cooking is my profession, I use these items regularly. However, many cooks do not use herbs and spices as frequently, and they go stale. In general, herbs and spices should be discarded after a year.

Spice and seasoning blends help reduce waste and expense. Look for blends that fit the "theme" of your recipe, then use an equivalent measure of the blend in place of the combination of herbs and seasonings called for. Example: Many Mexican recipes call for cumin and chili powder. Taco seasoning contains both spices, plus salt and other spices, and is a good replacement.

Must have:

- Salt: I prefer sea salt to regular iodized salt. (Once you get used to the flavor of sea salt, standard salt tastes overly chemical.) I use finely ground sea salt in recipes and use coarse salt when boiling water for pasta, rice or potatoes, or in recipes where I enjoy the crunch of the chunky salt. Coarse kosher salt also is a good choice.
- Pepper: I always use freshly ground black pepper. A good quality peppermill is an investment that will last a lifetime, and the flavor of the freshly ground pepper is far better than the pre-ground variety.
- Spice blends: Italian herbs, Cajun, taco seasoning and Old Bay are good starting points and eliminate the need for multiple containers of single spices.
- Spices and herbs: Savory - garlic salt and garlic powder, oregano, thyme, tarragon, cayenne pepper, paprika, bay leaves and rosemary. Sweet - cinnamon, nutmeg and cloves.

Other must-have seasonings:

- Soy sauce
- Worcestershire sauce
- Tabasco sauce
- Honey
- Vinegar: red wine and cider.

Occasional use:

- Spices and herbs: basil, crushed red pepper flakes, dry mustard, curry powder, chili powder, ginger, white pepper and cumin.
- Vinegar: red and white balsamic and rice wine.

A Well-Stocked Freezer and Refrigerator

A well-stocked pantry can save the day when trying to get dinner on the table quickly. But the supplies you stock in your refrigerator and freezer are the core of most meals.

Keeping the pantry stocked is simple, as most items have a long shelf life. Stocking your refrigerator and freezer takes a bit more attention and planning. I tend to keep a well-stocked freezer, which I supplement with more perishable items like fresh produce and dairy products. When chicken breast halves (bone-in or boneless) go on sale, I stock up and divide them into freezer bags for future meals. The same goes for pork tenderloin.

My freezer list is divided by category, and like my pantry list, was mostly culled from the ingredients from *The Quick Cooking with Karin Calloway Cookbook*.

While I do keep a bevy of frozen vegetables on hand, there are times when I prefer fresh. Frozen chopped onions and bell peppers are fine in a stew or long-simmered dish, but are on the soggy side in stir fries. There are other vegetables that I prefer fresh, like carrots and summer squash, which only take a few minutes to wash and slice or chop.

Your well-stocked freezer

MEATS

- Chicken: Boneless chicken breast halves (either the individually quick frozen breast halves you find in the freezer section, or sale chicken breast halves that I've repackaged in freezer bags in family-sized servings.) Chicken tenderloin fillets also are nice to have on hand.
- Pork tenderloin
- Ground beef: Both raw, formed into patties for burgers and pre-browned
- Stew beef
- Steaks
- Frozen meatballs: These have an occasional presence in my freezer, but can be a lifesaver on a hectic evening.
- Ground bulk pork sausage: preferably pre-browned
- Peeled and deveined frozen uncooked shrimp
- Bacon (Since this is an item we only serve occasionally, I like to keep it in the freezer.)
- Reduced fat kielbasa or Polish sausage (Turns chicken and rice into Jambalaya, or can be the centerpiece of your meal when grilled or sautéed.)
- Diced ham or ham steaks

VEGETABLES

- Seasoning blend: This combination of chopped onion, celery, bell pepper and parsley is a great time saver.
- Chopped onion
- Chopped green bell pepper (This can be a money saver when bell peppers are expensive in the winter months.)
- Peas
- Chopped spinach
- Creamed spinach (More than a side dish, I use creamed spinach as a pizza and pasta sauce, and as an addition to a simple but elegant Chicken Florentine, see page 49.)
- Mixed vegetables
- Southern-style hash brown potatoes

BREADS, PASTA AND OTHER ITEMS

- Pizza crusts
- Bread and roll dough
- Biscuits (The freezer variety taste better than the refrigerated biscuits in a tube.)
- Cheese ravioli and tortellini
- Pecans (They last longer in the freezer, and I always have some on hand for baking.)
- Ice cream
- Orange juice concentrate
- Pink Lemonade (It's a nice, quick beverage to offer guests.)

tocking your refrigerator takes a bit more planning, since items are perishable. In general, plan your menus for the week and purchase only the refrigerator items you will consume that week. Some items, like prepared salad dressings and marinades, will last for several months. But fresh vegetables and dairy products are best used right away.

Note: The starred (*) items are those that I keep on hand, then purchase the other items when I plan to use them.

Your well-stocked refrigerator

In the vegetable bin:
- Carrots*
- Celery*
- Onion*
- Fresh parsley*
- Lemons and/or limes*
- Lettuce: A head of leafy green lettuce, or bagged salad greens
- Bagged spinach
- Green onions
- Mushrooms
- Red bell peppers
- Fresh herbs (These have a very short storage period, and are best bought and used the same day.)

In the meat drawer:
- Several varieties of cheese*, both hunk and shredded: Parmesan, cheddar, mozzarella, feta, and Mexican blend
- Regular or reduced fat cream cheese
- Flour tortillas* (These also can be kept in the freezer.)
- Sliced deli meats (Sandwiches for lunch, or sometimes for dinner.)

Items you store in the door:
- Canned chopped garlic (I prefer freshly pressed or minced in most dishes, but this comes in handy in a pinch.)
- Reduced-fat mayonnaise*
- Dijon and regular yellow mustard*
- Ketchup*
- Prepared horseradish* (Combine with ketchup for cocktail sauce.)
- Mango chutney (This item can be stored in the pantry until opened. It's great over cream cheese and served with crackers as a spur-of-the-moment hors d'oeuvre!)
- Dale's Marinade* (This also can be stored in the pantry until opened.)
- Stir-fry sauce

- Sesame oil* (This oil is extremely perishable and lasts much longer when stored in the refrigerator. Just a small amount adds wonderful flavor to stir fries and other Oriental dishes.)
- Ranch dressing* (My daughter's favorite dressing is also great as a dip with fresh vegetables. It also can be tossed with diced raw potatoes and popped into a 350-degree oven for 45 minutes to an hour for a tasty side dish.)
- Other prepared dressings (We like to toss our salads with a simple dressing of garlic salt, red wine vinegar and olive oil, but keep your favorite dressings on hand for quick marinades and great salads.)
- Vanilla* (I used to store this in the pantry until Betty Powell, a wonderful Augusta cook, told me it maintains its flavor better when stored in the fridge.)

Other items:
- Milk*
- Eggs*
- Other dairy products: Half and half, ricotta or cottage cheese
- Pie crusts
- Tubes of crescent roll dough or pizza crust
- Fresh fish (I shop for fish on the day I plan to use it, and rarely purchase fish on Sunday. Most stores receive their weekend delivery of fresh fish on Friday, so you'll get fresher fish if you wait until the new delivery arrives on Monday. Get to know your seafood department manager. They offer a wealth of information on preparing your "catch" and also can tell you what is the freshest.)

Items that I keep on hand, but that don't fit into the pantry, refrigerator or freezer lists:
- Fresh tomatoes* (The flavor of fresh tomatoes is best when they are stored at room temperature.)
- Baking potatoes
- Bar items: Dry sherry, Bourbon, and red and white wine show up in a few of my recipes. (Since wine goes sour quickly after it's opened, you can eliminate waste by purchasing small "single serving" bottles in four-packs.)
- Bread products: Sandwich bread,* hamburger buns and good crusty French bread

Barb's Cheeseburger Pie   *page 76*

Menu Planning Pointers

Before you run to stock up at the store, let's back up and spend a little time on a game plan. After all, having ingredients on hand will help you solve the "what's for dinner?" dilemma, and you'll save money, time and pantry space by setting aside a little time each week for menu planning.

FIVE QUICK COOKING MENU-PLANNING POINTERS

■ Make a plan: I generally plan five meals a week, allowing for a night of takeout or restaurant dining and a night for leftovers.

Take some time on Sunday afternoon to map out your family's week, then match your menus according to the schedule. (No need to plan your most elaborate meal when everyone is running in different directions for meetings, practices or sports events.)

■ Take an inventory: Before you sit down to plan the week's menus, take an inventory of your pantry, refrigerator and freezer. Try to incorporate what you already have on hand into your menus.

■ Dinner on a plate: When planning your weekly menus, don't feel like everything has to be made from scratch! I call it the "dinner on a plate" philosophy, in which entrées such as spaghetti (boil water, cook pasta, heat sauce, toss bagged salad greens with dressing, heat prepared garlic bread) count as home-prepared meals. (If the dinner is mostly prepared at home, and you serve it on a plate, it counts!) When you buy into my "dinner on a plate" philosophy of family meal preparation, planning five dinners a week at home isn't as much of a chore as it sounds.

■ One recipe per meal: Don't overwhelm yourself by trying to incorporate three new recipes into one meal. Choose one course that requires a recipe, then fill in the menu with no-recipe items. No-recipe items include baked potatoes, packaged rice mixes, bagged salad greens, bottled dressings and frozen or fresh vegetables. Keep your menus simple during the week, and save the multi-recipe meals for the weekends or when entertaining.

■ Double-up for dual function: If you're serving meat sauce with spaghetti one night, brown extra ground beef and freeze it for another time. You won't dirty up another pan, and you'll love having the extra browned beef to use in another recipe. The same goes for cooked chicken.

Plan your menus to include "planned leftovers." A crockpot pork roast can become pulled-pork sandwiches later in the week. Leftover pot roast can become shepherd's pie. Extra meatballs in spaghetti sauce can be meatball subs the second time around. Grill extra chicken breasts for salads and casseroles.

Hot Turkey Salad   *page 51*

TABLE OF CONTENTS

1

Boursin Cheese Spread

appetizers

Boursin Cheese Spread

This creamy herbed cheese spread appeared in my first cookbook, and has been included again because it's so versatile. It's also used to sauce a delicious chicken, broccoli and pasta entrée on page 57. If you can't find the Fines Herbes, a spice blend that includes thyme, oregano, sage, rosemary, marjoram and basil, substitute an equal amount of Herbes de Provence or Italian Seasoning. This spread is a wonderful sandwich spread, too!

1 teaspoon minced garlic (1 large clove)
16 ounces cream cheese, softened*
1 cup butter, softened* (2 sticks)
2 teaspoons Fines Herbes
$1/4$ teaspoon dried dill weed
$1/4$ teaspoon freshly ground black pepper
$1/2$ teaspoon salt

Whip all ingredients in a food processor or with a hand mixer in a medium bowl, until smooth.

Makes $2^1/2$ cups.

*You can create a lower-fat spread by substituting three 8-ounce hunks of reduced-fat cream cheese for the cream cheese and butter.

Creamy Tomato Fondue

Creamy Tomato Fondue

Fondue was a fad in the '70s, and it's back in vogue again. I came up with this updated Tomato Fondue that's perfect for entertaining at home, poolside or anywhere! Reduce preparation time by using frozen chopped onion, minced garlic from a jar and bagged shredded cheese. Keep the dip warm in your fondue pot, and have plenty of bagel chips or toasted French bread rounds for dipping.

1 tablespoon olive oil
1 medium onion, chopped
1 teaspoon minced garlic (1 large clove)
1 28-ounce can diced tomatoes seasoned with basil, garlic and oregano.
1 cup dry white wine
16 ounces reduced-fat or regular cream cheese, cut into 1-inch cubes
1 cup shredded Monterey Jack cheese
Chopped fresh basil, for garnish
Toasted French bread rounds or cubes or bagel chips, for dipping

Heat the olive oil in a large skillet over medium. Add the onion and garlic and sauté until onion is very soft, about 8 minutes. Add the diced tomatoes and wine. Increase heat to medium-high and simmer 10 minutes, until liquid is almost completely reduced. Reduce heat to medium-low, add the cheeses and heat, stirring constantly, until melted. Pour into a fondue pot and keep warm over low heat.

Makes 12 appetizer servings.

Hot Clam Dip

I always keep a secret stash of quick hors d'oeuvres ingredients in my refrigerator and pantry. Two items that are usually on hand: a hunk of cream cheese and a can of clams. Here, the two combine in a sublime hot dip.

8 ounces cream cheese, softened
$1/2$ cup mayonnaise
$1/2$ cup sour cream
1 tablespoon prepared horseradish
2 teaspoons Worcestershire sauce
1 teaspoon minced garlic (1 large clove)
Hot pepper sauce, to taste
1 10.5-ounce can minced clams, drained
Crackers, pita chips, bagel chips or rippled
  potato chips

Hot Clam Dip

Preheat oven to 350 degrees. Stir together all ingredients except clams until well blended. Fold in clams and pour into a baking dish. Bake for 20 to 30 minutes, until bubbly.

Makes 12 appetizer servings.

Mediterranean Pizzas

Mediterranean Pizzas

Tortillas are good for more than burritos and sandwich wrappers. They crisp up into a delicious, thin pizza crust in this Mediterranean-inspired appetizer. Bake them up on cookie sheets, cut into wedges and watch them disappear!

Olive oil
4 7-inch flour tortillas
2 Roma tomatoes, thinly sliced
12 black Greek olives, pitted and sliced
3 ounces goat cheese, such as Montrachet, crumbled
1 tablespoon chopped fresh oregano or basil
Freshly ground black pepper, to taste

Preheat oven to 500 degrees. Brush two baking sheets with olive oil. Place two tortillas on each sheet. Divide tomatoes, olives, cheese and oregano among the tortillas. Drizzle each tortilla with a bit of olive oil, sprinkle with some black pepper and bake for 5 minutes, until tortillas are crisp. Cut each tortilla into wedges and serve.

Makes 8 appetizer servings.

Olive Bread

Stocking frozen bread dough in your freezer nets you more than loaves of bread. Once thawed, the dough can become pizza crust, cinnamon roll dough or this delicious stuffed-bread appetizer. Use a cherry pitter to easily remove the olive pits, or substitute pitted ripe black and green olives for the imported olives in the recipe.

Olive Bread

1 loaf frozen white bread dough, defrosted overnight in the refrigerator, or 1 10-ounce package refrigerated pizza dough
2 tablespoons butter spread flavored with garlic and olive oil, melted
$^{1}/_{4}$ cup green Spanish olives, pitted and sliced
$^{1}/_{4}$ cup pitted black Greek olives, pitted and sliced
1 cup shredded Mozzarella cheese or Italian Cheese blend
1 teaspoon olive oil
1 teaspoon fresh rosemary, chopped
1 teaspoon coarse sea salt

Let the bread or pizza crust dough sit at room temperature 30 minutes to one hour before proceeding with the recipe. This will give the gluten in the dough time to relax and will make rolling the dough easier.

Preheat oven to 400 degrees. Roll the dough into a 12-inch by 12-inch square. Brush the dough with the melted garlic butter. Place the olives down the center of the dough. Top with the cheese. Fold the left side over the filling, and then fold the right side over the top. Place the loaf on a parchment-lined baking sheet. Brush with the olive oil and sprinkle with the fresh rosemary and coarse sea salt. Bake for 25 to 30 minutes. Slice into 1-inch pieces before serving.

Makes 12 appetizer servings.

Quick Tip:

Look for butter spread flavored with garlic and olive oil in your supermarket's dairy case. The spread provides great garlic flavor, and often additional minced garlic is not needed. Use the spread to sauté meats and vegetables for great garlic flavor.

MB's Chip Dip!

Middle-schooler Mary Bryson Stuckey was one of my students during my summer 2003 cooking classes. An expert at cooking eggs, omelets and many other things, she's developed a number of her own recipes and shared her quick and delicious hot refried bean dip recipe with me. Thanks, Mary Bryson, for letting me include it here!

1 16-ounce can refried beans
10 tablespoons prepared salsa
1 teaspoon garlic or onion powder
1 cup shredded Monterrey Jack or cheddar cheese
Chips (Corn, tortilla, pita or even wavy potato chips)

Place refried beans in a microwave-safe bowl. Stir in the salsa and the garlic or onion powder. Sprinkle with the cheese. Microwave for 2 minutes, stir. Microwave for 2 minutes more. Serve with your favorite dipping chips.

Makes 8 appetizer servings.

Hot Artichoke Spread

This hot artichoke spread is ever-present at Augusta cocktail parties. The variations of this base recipe are endless, and I've given you three below.

1 14.5-ounce can quartered artichoke hearts, drained
$^1/_2$ cup reduced-fat mayonnaise
$^1/_2$ cup reduced-fat sour cream
1 cup shredded Parmesan cheese
Tabasco sauce, to taste (about 3 to 6 dashes)
Saltine or Table Water Crackers

Preheat oven to 350 degrees.
Chop artichoke hearts and place in a medium bowl.
Stir in mayonnaise, sour cream, Parmesan cheese and Tabasco sauce.
Spread in a glass baking dish. Bake for 30 minutes, until bubbly.
Serve with crackers.

Makes 12 appetizer servings.

Hot Artichoke Spread

Variations:

•• Chili, Cheese and Artichoke Dip: Substitute shredded cheddar cheese for the Parmesan and add one 4-ounce can of diced green chiles. Serve with corn or tortilla chips.

•• Elegant Seafood and Artichoke Spread: Double the original recipe and add an 8-ounce can of lump crabmeat and $^1/_4$ pound of cooked, chopped shrimp, one 4-ounce can of diced green chiles and a 2-ounce jar of diced pimentos. Serve with bagel or pita chips.

•• Spinach and Artichoke Dip: Substitute shredded Monterrey Jack cheese for the Parmesan, and add a package of defrosted, frozen creamed spinach to the remaining ingredients. Serve with tortilla chips. (Stouffer's and Bird's Eye are brands of frozen creamed spinach found in most supermarkets. Look for the Stouffer's with the frozen entrees and the Bird's Eye in the frozen vegetable section.)

Bacon-Wrapped Scallops

Seafood hors d'oeuvres are always impressive, and these delicious Bacon-Wrapped Scallops couldn't be easier to prepare. Using pre-cooked bacon slices to wrap the scallops saves time, and ensures that you don't overcook your scallops while waiting for the bacon to crisp.

1 pound fresh medium sea scallops
1 package pre-cooked bacon slices
Teriyaki baste and glaze

Preheat oven to 400 degrees. Line a baking sheet with aluminum foil and spray with nonstick cooking spray.

Wrap each scallop with a piece of the pre-cooked bacon and secure with a toothpick. Brush both sides with the baste and glaze. Bake for 10 to 15 minutes, until the scallops are done and the bacon is crisp.

Makes 6 appetizer servings.

Chicken Quesadillas

My children adore these quick Chicken Quesadillas for dinner, but they're also a wonderful hors d'oeuvre. Just cut the quesadillas into quarters, and top each serving with dollops of sour cream and salsa. A sprig of fresh cilantro will add the perfect finishing touch.

4 fajita-sized flour tortillas
3 chicken breast tenderloin filets (about $1/3$ pound of chicken)
1 teaspoon taco seasoning
$1/2$ cup shredded reduced-fat sharp cheddar cheese
Nonstick cooking spray
Sour cream, salsa and sprigs of fresh cilantro,
   if desired, for garnish

Remove the tortillas from the plastic wrapper and set aside to allow the tortillas to come to room temperature.

Spray a small nonstick skillet with cooking spray and heat over medium-high heat. Add the chicken breast tenders and sprinkle with the taco seasoning. Cook, turning several times, until chicken is done, about 6 minutes. Remove to a cutting board and chop coarsely.

Lay a tortilla on a flat surface or plate and sprinkle with $1/8$ cup of the cheese. Top with half of the chicken and another $1/8$ cup of cheese. Place another tortilla on top. Repeat with remaining tortillas, cheese and chicken.

Heat a skillet (large enough to hold a tortilla) that has been sprayed with the nonstick cooking spray over medium-high heat. Add one of the prepared quesadillas and cook until browned nicely, 2 to 3 minutes. Spray top tortilla with nonstick cooking spray and use a large spatula to flip the quesadilla to the other side. Cook 2 to 3 minutes. Remove from skillet and slice into quarters. Repeat with remaining quesadillas.

Makes 8 appetizer servings or 2 main dish servings.

Chicken Quesadillas

Smoked Sausage "Jezebel"

Smoked Sausage "Jezebel"

Little smoked sausages in barbecue sauce are ever present at casual parties. I've come up with a more elegant version that is sure to become a classic at your parties. The recipe replaces the little smoked sausages with sliced smoked sausage, and the barbecue sauce is replaced with a simple Jezebel sauce.

1 pound reduced-fat smoked sausage,
   sliced into $1/2$-inch rounds
1 8-ounce can pineapple tidbits packed
   in pineapple juice, undrained
4 ounces apple jelly ($1/2$ cup)
1 tablespoon Dijon mustard
1 tablespoon prepared horseradish

Brown sausage slices in a large nonstick skillet over medium-high heat, turning once. Add remaining ingredients. Bring to a boil, reduce heat and simmer for 15 minutes. Pour into a chafer, fondue pot or slow cooker and serve hot with toothpicks.

Makes 12 appetizer servings.

Creamy Black Bean Dip

I came up with this quick and tasty dip when I grew bored with regular salsa and tortilla chips. Jalapeño-Jack cheese gives the dip a kick, but you can use cheddar or Monterrey Jack if you have them on hand. A small can of shoe peg corn, well drained, is a nice addition to the dip.

Creamy Black Bean Dip

2 cups reduced-fat sour cream
1 tablespoon taco seasoning
$1/2$ teaspoon chili powder
$1/2$ teaspoon garlic salt
3 dashes Tabasco sauce
1 cup shredded Jalapeño-Jack or sharp cheddar cheese
1 15-ounce can black beans, rinsed and drained
1 4-ounce can diced green chiles
1 green onion, chopped

Combine sour cream, taco seasoning, chili powder, garlic salt and Tabasco in a medium bowl. Fold in cheese, black beans, green chiles and chopped green onion. Refrigerate until ready to serve.

Makes 12 appetizer servings.

Marinated Shrimp

Marinated Shrimp

The judge of a good party often isn't the ambience of the setting or the graciousness of the hosts. In all honesty, what's often remembered most is a bountiful supply of shrimp. While good steamed shrimp with zesty cocktail sauce are always a hit, this simple marinated shrimp hors d'oeuvres takes steamed shrimp to another level. Buying in-store peeled, deveined and steamed shrimp saves you a lot of preparation time.

2 pounds medium to large shrimp, cooked, peeled and deveined
1 medium onion, thinly sliced
4 bay leaves
$1/2$ cup extra virgin olive oil
1 tablespoon white balsamic or white wine vinegar
1 3.5-ounce jar capers, undrained
2 teaspoons Worcestershire sauce
$1/4$ teaspoon hot pepper sauce, or less to taste

Combine all ingredients in a zip-top plastic bag and marinate 8 to 24 hours. Pour into a bowl and serve with toothpicks.

Makes 10 appetizer servings.

Nine-Layer Mediterranean Spread

Everyone loves layered dips, and this one has a decidedly Mediterranean accent. Caponata — a canned product which combines roasted eggplant, bell peppers, onion and spices — can be found in the canned vegetable aisle in some supermarkets. If your supermarket doesn't carry it, substitute chopped, roasted red bell peppers, which are readily available.

8 ounces reduced-fat cream cheese
4 ounces crumbled Feta cheese
1 tablespoon Italian seasoning
1 cup shredded Parmesan cheese
1 7.5-ounce can Caponata (Eggplant appetizer)
1 green onion, finely chopped
1 4-ounce can chopped black olives, drained
1 8-ounce jar marinated artichoke hearts, drained and chopped
Pita or bagel chips or crackers

Combine cream cheese, crumbled Feta and Italian seasonings in a food processor or with a hand mixer in a medium bowl. Set aside.

Line a 1-quart bowl with plastic wrap, allowing 8 inches of wrap to extend over sides of the bowl. Layer ingredients in this order: $1/2$ of the Parmesan, $1/2$ of the Caponata, $1/2$ of the cream cheese mixture, the green onions, olives, artichoke hearts, remaining Caponatta, remaining cream cheese, remaining Parmesan. Fold plastic wrap over top and chill until firm. Serve with pita chips or crackers.

Makes 12 appetizer servings

Nine-Layer Mediterranean Spread

Variations:

Create two more delicious layered spreads in a snap. Here's how!

•• Layered Smoked Salmon Spread: Line bowl as indicated above, then layer with: $1/2$ cup finely chopped red onion; one 3.5-ounce jar capers, drained; 2 hard-cooked eggs, chopped; 4 ounces smoked salmon, chopped. Combine 8 ounces reduced-fat cream cheese and 2 teaspoons dried dill weed and spread over top. Serve with toast points.

•• Layered Chutney Spread: Line bowl as indicated above, then layer with $1/3$ cup roasted peanuts, chopped; 2 green onions, chopped; and one 8-ounce can crushed pineapple, drained well. Combine 8 ounces reduced-fat cream cheese and 1 teaspoon curry powder and spread over top. Top with $1/2$ cup chopped mango chutney. Serve with round buttery crackers, such as Ritz.

Shrimp Sizzlers

We've all heard the phrase "saving for a rainy day." While the saying refers to saving money for an unexpected need, my rainy day stash is hors d'oeuvres in the freezer for unexpected guests. These delicious little shrimp rolls can be prepared weeks in advance, then baked just before serving.

1 tablespoon butter or margarine, plus $\frac{1}{4}$ cup, melted
1 pound medium shrimp, peeled and deveined
1 green onion, chopped
$\frac{1}{4}$ cup grated cheddar cheese
2 tablespoons grated Parmesan cheese
3 ounces cream cheese, softened
1 tablespoon Sherry, optional
14 slices soft white bread, crust removed

Melt 1 tablespoon butter in a medium skillet.
Add shrimp and chopped green onion, and saute until shrimp are completely cooked, about 2 minutes.
Set aside to cool.

When shrimp are cool, place the shrimp and onion in the bowl of a food processor fitted with a metal blade. Pulse several times to chop shrimp. Add cheeses and sherry and pulse several times, just until mixture is blended.

Use a rolling pin to flatten out the slices of bread. Spread 2 tablespoons of the shrimp mixture on each bread slice and roll up tightly. Brush with the melted butter and place on a parchment paper-lined baking sheet. Cover baking sheet with plastic wrap or foil. Chill rolls for 1 hour or freeze.

Preheat oven to 425 degrees. Cut frozen rolls into 4 small rounds and arrange them on a parchment-lined baking sheet, seam side down. Bake until golden, about 15 minutes. Cool slightly before serving.

Makes 56 Sizzlers.

Shrimp Sizzlers

Quick Tip:

When time is really short, substitute crab spread from your supermarket in place of the shrimp mixture. Leftover spinach or artichoke spread and even pimento cheese spread are also wonderful fillings.

Variation:

• • Asparagus Roll-Ups: Spread the flattened bread slices with a filling of 3 ounces of softened cream cheese mixed with 3 ounces of crumbled blue cheese and 1 egg. Drain a can of asparagus spears and place a spear on top of each bread slice before rolling up tightly. Brush the rolls with melted butter and freeze on a cookie sheet. Then, pop them in a freezer bag to bake later. When ready to bake, follow the directions for the shrimp sizzlers and cut each roll into four pieces and bake at 425 degrees for 15 minutes.

Quick Appetizers
from a Hunk of Cream Cheese

I've often written and talked about cream cheese as a lifesaver when whipping up quick appetizers for planned or unplanned guests. Here are some of my favorite ways to turn a block of cream cheese into something special!

Quick:

- Spread softened cream cheese on slices of boiled ham, top with a bud of pickled okra or a dill pickle wedge, roll up and slice into 1-inch bites. Skewer each roll with a toothpick and place on a platter. Or, spread the softened cream cheese on smoked salmon slices, roll up, slice and serve garnished with tiny caper berries or chopped green onion.

- Mix softened cream cheese with a tin of drained smoked oysters, a dash of Worcestershire, a bit of minced garlic or garlic powder and a tablespoon of mayonnaise. Spread in a pretty bowl and serve with saltine or table water crackers.

- Combine your hunk of cream cheese with a package of Knorr Vegetable Soup Mix and 10 ounces of defrosted, well drained frozen spinach. Add three chopped green onions and $1/2$ cup sour cream. Serve as is, cold, or stir in 1 cup of shredded Monterey Jack cheese, spread in an 8-inch square glass baking dish and bake for 20 to 30 minutes, until bubbly.

Quicker:

- Spread your hunk of cream cheese on a plate and top with cocktail sauce and sprinkle liberally with drained canned crab or cocktail shrimp. Serve with crackers.

- Spread your cream cheese in a glass bread pan, top with salsa or canned chili and sprinkle with some grated cheese and microwave for 3 minutes, until cheese is melted. Serve with tortilla chips.

- Spread your cream cheese in a glass pie plate, top with 1 cup of pizza sauce, shredded mozzarella and sliced pepperoni and microwave until bubbly. Serve with corn chips.

Quickest:

- Plop a hunk of cream cheese on a pretty plate and top with hot pepper jelly, Dr. Pete's Praline Mustard Glaze (available in specialty food stores) or leftover cranberry sauce. Spread on buttery crackers.

2

Chilled Avocado-Lime Soup

soups

Chilled Avocado-Lime Soup

Winter is usually thought of as soup season. But, a cold soup in the summer can be a refreshing change of pace. My Avocado-Lime Soup is lusciously rich and simple to prepare. For a pretty and fun table setting, I like to serve the soup in martini glasses along with some quickly prepared turkey tortilla wraps. To prepare the wraps, just spread herb and garlic-seasoned cream cheese on flour tortillas, then layer with deli turkey, lettuce leaves and diced tomato. Or, make this soup the centerpiece of a summer meal by topping it with cooked and peeled shrimp, lump crabmeat or shredded chicken, and serve some tortilla chips on the side.

3 ripe avocados
1 cup reduced-fat sour cream
1 14.5-ounce can reduced-sodium chicken broth, chilled
Juice of 2 limes
Salt and freshly ground black pepper, to taste

$^1/_2$ teaspoon chili powder, optional
Dash Tabasco
Diced avocado, optional, for garnish
Diced fresh tomato, optional, for garnish

Place all ingredients except optional garnishes in a blender or food processor and blend until smooth. Pour the soup into serving bowls, or refrigerate until ready to serve. Top each serving with some diced avocado and tomato, if desired.

Makes 8 servings.

Quick tip:

I always use fresh lime and lemon juice. Bottled juice tastes overly acidic to me, and the only substitute I'll make is the frozen lemon juice you'll find in your grocer's freezer alongside the orange juice concentrate. Get the most juice from your citrus fruits by microwaving them for 20 to 30 seconds. Then, roll the fruit on the counter, pressing down with the palm of your hand. This breaks up the inner fibers, giving you more juice. A plastic or wooden lemon reamer is a helpful kitchen gadget, but the tines of a salad fork also can be used to juice citrus fruits.

Tomato-Okra Gumbo

Tomato-Okra Gumbo

Cans of Rotel tomatoes, corn and frozen okra become a hearty vegetarian gumbo that I like to serve on busy nights, year-round. Serve over cooked white rice with some corn muffins (home-baked from a mix or purchased in your supermarket's bakery), and you've got a quick, healthy meal.

2 10-ounce cans mild Rotel tomatoes, undrained
1 15-ounce can whole kernel corn, drained
1 16-ounce bag frozen sliced okra
3 cups cooked white rice

Place Rotel tomatoes and corn in a saucepan and bring to a boil. Stir in the okra and simmer 10 minutes. Place a scoop of rice in each bowl and top with the gumbo.

Makes 6 servings.

Bean, Bacon and Chicken Soup

This recipe is similar to my White Chili, a popular recipe in my first cookbook, but it's a bit heartier. My husband and children enjoy this soup immensely when I serve it with some garlic-cheese biscuits and a big tossed salad. When you're ready to serve, just garnish your soup with some freshly grated Romano cheese and diced chopped tomato, if desired.

6 slices thick-cut bacon, diced
1 medium onion, chopped (about 1 cup)
1 medium carrot, peeled and grated
2 boneless, skinless chicken breast halves,
   cut into 1-inch pieces
1 teaspoon minced garlic (1 large clove)
1 bay leaf
32 ounces reduced-sodium chicken broth (4 cups)
2 15-ounce cans white beans, rinsed and drained
2 cups coarsely chopped fresh spinach
Freshly grated Romano cheese, for garnish, optional
1 small tomato, diced, for garnish, optional

Sauté bacon in a Dutch oven over medium heat until crisp. Remove with a slotted spoon, reserving bacon for later. Pour out all but 1 tablespoon of the bacon drippings. Heat over medium-high. Add the onion, carrot, chicken and garlic and sauté until the onion is tender and the chicken almost cooked through, about 4 minutes. Add the bay leaf, chicken broth and white beans. Bring to a boil, reduce heat and simmer 30 minutes.

Add the chopped spinach and reserved bacon to the soup and heat until the spinach is wilted, about 3 minutes. Serve in bowls, garnished with the grated Romano cheese and diced tomatoes, if desired.

Makes 8 servings.

Quick tip:

This soup can be lightened up a great deal by omitting the bacon, then sautéing the onion and diced chicken in olive oil. Or, simply spray your soup pot with nonstick cooking spray and skip the added fat all together.

Bean, Bacon and Chicken Soup

• •Vegetarian Variation:
For a tasty vegetarian version, omit both the bacon and chicken, and replace the chicken broth with vegetable broth.

Beef, Wild Rice and Mushroom Soup

One of my favorite soups is a wild rice and mushroom soup that's loaded with heavy cream. It's the perfect first course for a dinner party, but too rich for family fare. While seeking to replicate the flavor without all the fat, I came up with this Beef, Wild Rice and Mushroom Soup. The beef takes the soup from starter to main course, while evaporated skim milk lends rich flavor without adding all those fat grams.

This soup is also wonderful when leftover Thanksgiving turkey or rotisserie chicken replace the beef, and reduced-sodium chicken broth is substituted for the beef broth.

Beef, Wild Rice and Mushroom Soup

1 tablespoon vegetable oil or nonstick cooking spray
1 pound stew beef, cut into 1-inch pieces
Salt and freshly ground black pepper
2 tablespoons all-purpose flour
2 14.5-ounce cans reduced-sodium beef broth

1 6-ounce package long grain and wild rice mix
8 ounces sliced fresh mushrooms
1 12-ounce can evaporated skim milk
1 tablespoon sherry, optional

Heat the oil in a Dutch oven over medium-high heat. Season the beef with salt and pepper and add to the hot pot. Sear on one side without stirring, about 2 minutes. Stir or turn beef pieces with tongs and sear on other side 2 minutes. Add flour, stir and cook 1 minute.

Add 1 cup of the broth, stirring well to dissolve the flour. Add remaining broth, rice mix and seasonings and sliced mushrooms. Bring mixture to a boil, reduce heat and simmer 20 to 25 minutes, until rice is tender. Stir in evaporated milk and continue cooking on low until heated through; do not boil. Taste, and adjust seasonings with additional salt and pepper. Stir in sherry if desired.

Makes 8 servings.

Quick Tip:

Many of my soups are quite hearty and are the perfect centerpiece for a casual family meal. Add a tossed salad and some good bread, and dinner is ready!

Black Bean Soup

My favorite black bean soup, from "Tea-Time at the Masters," started by soaking dried beans overnight, then cooking them for hours with a ham bone until the beans became tender. I've skipped the step and have substituted canned black beans and diced smoked ham for a quick, satisfying soup. If time is especially short, substitute a package of "seasoning blend" – a combination of onion, bell pepper and celery that can be found in the frozen vegetable section of most supermarkets – for the chopped onion, celery, leek and parsley in the recipe.

Black Bean Soup

1 tablespoon olive oil
1 cup cubed cooked lean smoked ham
1 medium onion, chopped (about 1 cup)
2-3 stalks celery, chopped (about 1 cup)
1 leek, white part only, chopped (about $^3/_4$ cup)
$^1/_2$ cup fresh parsley, finely chopped
1 tablespoon all-purpose flour
6 cups reduced-sodium chicken broth,
 water or a combination

3 16-ounce cans black beans, rinsed and drained
2 bay leaves
Salt and freshly ground black pepper, to taste
$^1/_4$ cup Madeira or sherry, optional
Sour cream, for garnish
Lemon slices, for garnish

Heat the olive oil in a large Dutch oven over medium-high heat. Add the ham, onion, celery, leeks and parsley. Sauté until onion is golden. Stir in the flour, then add the broth or water, whisking well until flour is dissolved.

Add the black beans and bay leaves and bring to a boil, reduce heat and simmer 20 to 30 minutes. Remove bay leaves and season to taste with salt and pepper. Puree soup slightly using an immersion blender, or mash some of the beans with a potato masher. Add the Madeira or sherry, if desired. Ladle into soup bowls and top with a dollop of sour cream and a slice of lemon.

Makes 8 servings.

Quick Tip:

Leeks add wonderful flavor to soups and are delicious on their own either braised or poached. Be careful when washing leeks, as they can be very sandy. Cut the leeks just above the white part and cut off the root end. Slice the leek in half lengthwise and you'll reveal the leek's inner layers – which are where the sand usually hides. Rinse the inside of each half with running water, then proceed with your recipe, either slicing or dicing the leek, or leaving it intact to be braised or poached.

Chicken Enchilada Soup

My favorite chicken enchiladas are a combination of diced chicken, sour cream, cheese and spinach, all wrapped in a flour tortilla and baked. While the combination is quite delicious, its preparation can be time consuming. I devised this recipe for Chicken Enchilada Soup as a way to satisfy my craving for the flavors of the dish without all the work.

2 tablespoons butter, margarine or olive oil
4 boneless, skinless chicken breast halves, diced
2 teaspoons minced garlic (about 2 large cloves)
1 4-ounce can diced green chiles
2 14.5-ounce cans reduced-sodium chicken broth
8 ounces reduced-fat sour cream
1 10³/₄-ounce can Chili Cheese Dip*
1 10-ounce package frozen chopped spinach,
    defrosted and drained well
1 cup reduced-fat shredded cheddar or Monterey Jack
    cheese, for garnish, optional

Chicken Enchilada Soup

Heat the butter, margarine or olive oil in a Dutch oven. Add the chicken and sauté 3 minutes. Add the garlic and sauté 3 minutes more, until chicken is nearly done. Add the diced green chiles and the chicken broth and bring to a boil. Reduce heat and stir in the sour cream, chili cheese dip and chopped spinach. Simmer 5 to 10 minutes, but DO NOT BOIL. Ladle into bowls and top each serving with some of the shredded cheese.

Makes 6 servings.

*Frito-Lay brand Chili Cheese Dip was used for testing purposes. Other brands of cheese dip or "con queso" may be substituted.

Minute Minestrone

How do you satisfy your family's craving for something hot and hearty on a busy weeknight? You could reach for the can opener and heat up a can of soup. But with about 30 minutes and a few ingredients you could whip up my recipe for Minute Minestrone. Add a loaf of crusty bread to complete your meal.

1¹/₂ cups frozen cheese tortellini
    (about ¹/₃ of a 19-ounce package)
8 ounces pork or turkey Italian sausage
¹/₂ cup chopped onion
2 14.5-ounce cans reduced-sodium beef broth
2 14.5-ounce cans diced tomatoes seasoned
    with basil, garlic and oregano
1 16-ounce package frozen vegetables
    (Roma blend or California blend)
1 16-ounce can Great Northern or Navy beans,
    rinsed and drained, optional

Bring a large pot of water to a boil. Add the tortellini and cook according to package directions. Drain and set aside.

While the pasta water boils, spray a Dutch oven with nonstick cooking spray. Crumble the sausage into the Dutch oven, add the onions and sauté over medium-high heat until the sausage is browned and the onions are golden. Drain the sausage and onions in a colander and return to the Dutch oven. Add the beef broth and tomatoes and bring to a boil. Add the frozen vegetables and beans, if desired. Reduce heat and simmer 10 to 12 minutes.

To serve, place some of the tortellini in the bottom of each soup bowl and ladle the soup over top.

Makes 6 servings.

Quick Tip:

My Minute Minestrone calls for cooking the tortellini separately so that the tortellini don't absorb all of the liquid if leftover soup were stored in the refrigerator. Go ahead and cook the tortellini in the soup if you don't anticipate leftovers! Just add the tortellini along with the frozen vegetables.

Quick Crab Chowder

I love the creamy bisques and chowders served in restaurants, and they're not difficult to re-create at home. With a few convenience products, and a can of crabmeat, you can enjoy a sublime seafood chowder any time.

1 tablespoon butter or margarine
1 16-ounce bag seasoning blend
1 10³/₄-ounce can condensed cream
  of potato soup
1 15-ounce can cream-style corn
Salt and freshly ground black pepper, to taste
¹/₂ teaspoon dried thyme
2 cups half and half
8 ounces lump or "special" pasteurized
  crabmeat, picked over for shells
¹/₂ cup chopped fresh parsley, for garnish
1 tablespoon dry sherry per serving, optional

Quick Crab Chowder

Melt butter in a Dutch oven over medium-high heat. Add the seasoning blend and sauté until the vegetables are tender. Add the soup, corn, seasonings and half and half and bring to a simmer. Add the crabmeat and simmer gently for 15 to 20 minutes. DO NOT BOIL. Ladle into bowls and sprinkle each serving with some of the chopped parsley and stir in a tablespoon of sherry, if desired.

Makes 6 servings.

Taco Stew

My friend Martha Long passed along this hearty cold-weather recipe. Martha calls it a soup, but I think it's more of a stew, since the only liquid comes from undrained cans of beans and corn. Martha says the "soup-stew" doesn't even require spoons. Simply serve with a bowl of tortilla or corn chips to scoop the soup from bowl to mouth.

1 pound lean ground beef
1 medium onion, chopped (about 1 cup)
1 bell pepper, chopped (about 1¹/₂ cups)
1 package taco seasoning
1 package powdered ranch dressing mix
1 teaspoon chili powder

1 16-ounce can pinto beans, undrained
1 16-ounce can kidney beans, undrained
1 11.5-ounce can Mexicorn, undrained
1 16-ounce can white hominy, drained
Tortilla or corn chips, as accompaniment

Sauté the ground beef in a Dutch oven over medium-high heat until browned. Drain in a colander. Sauté onions and green bell peppers in the pan while the meat drains. Return the meat to the pan and add remaining ingredients. Bring to a boil, then reduce heat and simmer 15 minutes.

Makes 8 servings.

Sweet Potato Soup

Sweet potatoes are an ever-present part of the Thanksgiving menu. But instead of serving them candied, mashed or baked into a sweet potato soufflé, why not consider serving a luscious Sweet Potato Soup? Whether you add the recipe to your Thanksgiving repertoire or serve it on a chilly fall evening, you'll love this soup's sweet-and-savory flavor and its simple preparation.

Nonstick cooking spray
1 medium onion, chopped (about 1 cup)
1 Granny Smith apple, peeled and grated
32 ounces reduced-sodium chicken broth (4 cups)

1 29-ounce can yams or sweet potatoes,
    packed in syrup, rinsed, drained and diced
1 teaspoon Pumpkin Pie Spice
Salt and freshly ground black pepper, to taste
Additional slivers of Granny Smith Apple,
    for garnish

Spray a Dutch oven with the cooking spray and heat over medium-high. Add onions and grated apple and sauté for 5 minutes. Add broth, yams or sweet potatoes, pumpkin pie spice and salt and pepper. Raise heat to high, cover and bring to a boil. Reduce heat to low and simmer, uncovered, for 15 to 20 minutes. Remove from the heat and puree with an immersion blender.* Ladle into bowls and garnish with the apple slivers.

Makes 6 servings.

*If you don't have an immersion blender, prepare the soup ahead and let it cool. Puree in the blender, and then reheat the soup over medium heat for 10 to 15 minutes.

Sweet Potato Soup

Quick Tip:

Use caution when pureeing hot liquids in a blender. The steam from the hot liquid can cause the top of the blender to pop off, spewing hot liquid and resulting in the potential to be burned. Never fill the blender more than $1/3$ full of a hot liquid.

Thai Coconut Chicken Soup

I love dining in Thai restaurants. Every dish has a unique combination of flavors – spicy, salty, sweet and savory – all in one plate or bowl. Thai Coconut Chicken Soup is available at most Thai restaurants, but I've come up with a recipe you can enjoy at home. Add a salad of peeled and sliced cucumbers tossed with seasoned rice wine vinegar and sprinkled with chopped peanuts, heat up some egg rolls from the freezer section, and enjoy a culinary trip to the Orient.

Thai Coconut Chicken Soup

2 14.5-ounce cans reduced-sodium chicken broth
4 ounces fresh ginger root, unpeeled and cut into 1-inch slices
1 lemon, peeled* and juiced
1 lime, peeled*
2 cans reduced-fat, unsweetened coconut milk**
1 pound boneless, skinless chicken breast halves,
    cut into thin strips
8 ounces sliced fresh mushrooms
2 tablespoons brown sugar
2 tablespoons fish sauce**
1 jalapeño pepper, sliced, or to taste

Combine broth, ginger and citrus peel in a Dutch oven or large saucepan and bring to a boil over medium-high heat. Add the coconut milk and return to a boil. Stir in the chicken strips, mushrooms, lemon juice, brown sugar and fish sauce and bring back to a boil. Reduce heat and simmer 3 minutes, until chicken is cooked. Stir in sliced jalapeños and serve.

Makes 8 servings.

*Use a vegetable peeler to remove long 1" strips of peel from the lemon and lime.
**Look for unsweetened coconut milk and fish sauce in the Oriental foods section of your supermarket.

Unrolled Cabbage Soup

Every year on New Year's Day I spend several hours preparing my family's traditional feast: Hungarian Cabbage Rolls. While I don't mind the work once a year, I've come up with my Unrolled Cabbage Soup as a way to quickly satisfy my craving for the dish. All you need to complete your meal is some good crusty bread for dipping. But, if you'd like to experience my family's true Hungarian tradition, serve with sides of potato salad and cucumber salad.

1 pound lean ground beef
1 medium onion, chopped (about 1 cup)
1 10-ounce package finely shredded cabbage
    for coleslaw (or 3 cups finely shredded green
    cabbage)
1 28-ounce can diced tomatoes, undrained
1 15-ounce can tomato sauce
32 ounces reduced-sodium chicken broth (4 cups)
1 cup cider vinegar
1 tablespoon sweet paprika
Salt and freshly ground black pepper, to taste
2 cups cooked white rice

Brown ground beef and onion in a Dutch oven over medium-high heat. Drain and return to the pan. Heat over medium-high and stir in the cabbage, tomatoes, tomato sauce, broth, vinegar and paprika. Bring to a boil, reduce heat and simmer 1 hour. Season to taste with salt and pepper. Place $1/4$ cup of the cooked rice in the bottom of each soup bowl, then ladle the soup over top.

Makes 8 servings.

Unrolled Cabbage Soup

Pazole Blanco

While White Chili has been the rage in the recipe world for the past few years, there's another warm stew with a Mexican accent that has equal merit. Pazole Blanco, with its combination of chicken, pork and hominy, is a hearty cold-weather main dish. I first sampled Pazole at the home of Ron and Eunice Fenchak, way back when I worked in public relations at the Medical College of Georgia. Eunice's elaborate preparation has been given a few shortcuts here, but the resulting dish will definitely warm you up during cool months.

Pazole Blanco

1 tablespoon olive oil
1 boneless, skinless chicken breast half, cubed
1 pound lean boneless pork chops, cubed
1 small onion, chopped (about $^1/_2$ cup)
1 teaspoon minced garlic (about 1 large clove)
$^1/_2$-1 teaspoon dried crushed red pepper flakes, to taste
Salt and freshly ground black pepper, to taste

32 ounces reduced-sodium chicken broth (4 cups)
1 15.5-ounce can golden hominy, rinsed and drained
Shredded lettuce, for garnish
Lime wedges, for garnish
Diced tomatoes, for garnish
Peeled and quartered avocado, for garnish

Heat olive oil in a large deep skillet or Dutch oven. Add chicken and pork pieces and brown, stirring occasionally, for 5 minutes. Add onions, garlic, red pepper flakes and salt and pepper and sauté until onions are translucent, 5 to 8 minutes. Add chicken broth, bring to a boil, reduce heat and simmer 15 minutes. Stir in hominy and simmer 10 minutes more. Serve in bowls, adding garnishes, as desired.

Makes 6 servings.

Cold Cucumber Yogurt Soup

Cold Cucumber Yogurt Soup

Cold Cream of Cucumber Soup, often called Cucumber Vichyssoise, was a popular cold soup during the 1950s. The classic recipe required a good bit of pre-planning. But my version comes together in minutes and requires little advanced preparation. Simply place all of the ingredients in the refrigerator before leaving the house in the morning, and throw everything into the blender when you return home. I like to serve the soup with tuna salad finger sandwiches, for a retro soup and sandwich supper.

1 10$^3/_4$-ounce can cream of potato soup
1 14.5-ounce can reduced-sodium chicken broth
1 8-ounce container nonfat plain yogurt

2 cups peeled and diced cucumber
   (about 1 English cucumber or 2 Kirby cucumbers)
1 teaspoon garlic salt
Freshly ground black pepper, to taste

Combine all ingredients in a blender or food processor and puree until smooth.
Serve immediately, or refrigerate until ready to serve.

Makes 8 servings.

Freezer-Aisle Corn Chowder

My Quick Corn Chowder, which appeared in my first cookbook, was an instant hit when the recipe ran in *The Augusta Chronicle*. Since frozen au gratin potatoes have become difficult to find now, I developed this recipe to take advantage of other frozen convenience products. Using these supermarket "finds" not only saves you time, but also allows you to create a rich and filling homemade soup. Using frozen

Freezer-Aisle Corn Chowder

stir-fry pepper blend, whole kernel corn and diced Southern-style hash brown potatoes keeps your time at the cutting board to a minimum! And the resulting dish is simply delicious.

3 slices bacon
1 cup frozen stir-fry pepper blend,
  thawed and coarsely chopped
1 rib celery, chopped
1 teaspoon minced garlic (1 large clove)
$^1/_4$ cup all-purpose flour
1 bay leaf
2 14.5-ounce cans reduced-sodium chicken broth

3 cups frozen Southern-style hash browns
  or peeled and diced fresh potatoes
2 cups frozen whole kernel corn
$^1/_2$ teaspoon dried thyme
1 teaspoon salt
$^1/_2$ teaspoon freshly ground black pepper
Dash cayenne pepper, optional
1 16-ounce can cream-style corn
1 cup whipping cream

Fry bacon in a Dutch oven over medium-high heat, until crisp. Remove and drain on paper towels.

Add stir-fry blend and celery to bacon drippings and sauté 2 to 3 minutes. Add garlic and sauté 1 minute. Add flour, stirring, 1 minute. Add bay leaf and 1 can of the chicken broth, stirring until smooth. Add remaining can of broth, diced potatoes, frozen corn,

thyme, salt, black pepper and cayenne, if desired. Cover and bring to a boil. Reduce heat and simmer, covered, 15 minutes. When potatoes are tender, stir in cream-style corn and whipping cream and heat through. DO NOT BOIL.

Makes 6 servings.

Quickest Clam Chowder

It doesn't take much more than a can opener to create this quick chowder!

1 $10^3/_4$-ounce can cream of potato soup
1 $10^3/_4$-ounce can cream of celery soup
1 cup milk
1 10.5-ounce cans minced or chopped clams, undrained
1 cup whipping cream or half and half

Combine soups and milk in a medium saucepan over medium heat. Bring to a boil, reduce heat and stir in the clams with their juices and the whipping cream or half and half. Heat through, but do not boil.

Makes 4 servings.

Squash Bisque

The inspiration for this luscious soup recipe came from a meal my husband, Bond, and I shared at a Southern family-style restaurant where we dined on platters of fried chicken and an amazing array of vegetable side dishes. The standout dish of the meal was simple summer squash, which was steamed with onions and a mystery ingredient – dried tarragon.

The flavor of the squash seasoned with the tarragon was a match made in heaven and a combination I'd never dreamed of. I've taken the two and combined them in this delicious Squash Bisque. Serve your bisque as a first course or as a light main dish with rolls and a salad.

2 tablespoons butter or margarine
1 medium onion, chopped (about 1 cup)
4 medium yellow squash, washed and diced
1 teaspoon minced garlic (1 large clove)
1 teaspoon dried tarragon
1 14.5-ounce can reduced-sodium chicken broth
$^1/_2$ cup whipping cream
Salt and freshly ground black pepper, to taste

Sauté the onion and squash in the butter or margarine in a Dutch oven over medium-high heat until the onions are transparent. Stir in the garlic and tarragon, and add the chicken broth. Bring to a boil, reduce heat and simmer 20 minutes, until squash is tender. Puree the bisque with an immersion blender*. Stir in the cream and season to taste with salt and freshly ground black pepper.

Makes 4 to 6 servings.

*The bisque can be cooled slightly and pureed in batches in a food processor or blender. Reheat in the Dutch oven before adding the whipping cream. Always use caution when puree-ing hot liquids in a blender.

Squash Bisque

Can-Can Tex-Mex Chowder

Open a couple of cans and a hot, spicy soup is on the table in just minutes!

1 8-ounce can cream-style corn
1 15-ounce can yellow corn, drained
1 10-ounce can Rotel tomatoes, undrained
1 15-ounce can black beans, rinsed and drained
1 14.5-ounce can reduced-sodium chicken broth
Shredded cheddar or Monterrey Jack cheese,
  for garnish
Sour cream, for garnish

Combine all canned ingredients in a medium saucepan over medium-high heat. Bring to a boil, reduce heat and simmer 5 to 10 minutes. Serve in bowls, garnishing each serving with shredded cheese and a dollop of sour cream.

Makes 4 servings.

3

Greek Tortellini Salad

salads

Greek Tortellini Salad

My Greek Tortellini Salad is a cooling side dish to accompany all your grilled entrées, or it can serve as an entrée salad. Take some along to your next cookout as a nice change of pace from your usual pasta salad.

1 9-ounce package refrigerated cheese tortellini, cooked according to package directions, drained well
5 Roma tomatoes, washed and cut into large chunks
$^1/_2$ English seedless cucumber, unpeeled, cut into large chunks
1 4-ounce can sliced black olives, drained
$^1/_4$ cup sliced mild pepperoncini peppers, drained
$^1/_2$ cup bottled reduced-fat Italian or Greek salad dressing
3 green onions, chopped
$^1/_4$ cup chopped fresh parsley
4 ounces crumbled reduced-fat feta cheese

Combine all ingredients in a large serving bowl.
Cover with plastic wrap and refrigerate for several hours or overnight, until well chilled.

Makes 10 side-dish servings.

Corn and Fettuccine Salad

Corn and Fettuccine Salad is my version of a salad bar favorite. My recipe comes close to the restaurant variety, can be whipped up in a snap and is a nice change of pace from deli potato salad at any picnic or cookout. This salad goes great with grilled burgers, steaks or chicken, so take it along anywhere you might have some cookout fun!

9 ounces refrigerated fettuccine, cooked according to package directions, drained and set aside
1 cup frozen corn niblets, defrosted and drained well
$^2/_3$ cups reduced-fat mayonnaise
$^1/_2$ cup grated Parmesan cheese
1 teaspoon garlic powder
1 teaspoon freshly ground black pepper
Salt, to taste

Corn and Fettuccine Salad

Combine pasta and corn in a large bowl. In a separate bowl, combine remaining ingredients. Fold mayonnaise mixture into fettuccine and corn. Season to taste with salt and more black pepper, if desired. Refrigerate several hours before serving.

Makes 10 side-dish servings.

Greek Salad

Greek Salad

Seafood is typical beach cuisine. But my annual trek to the beach isn't complete until I've had a Greek Salad. This salad is the signature dish of our summer vacation spot, New Smyrna Beach, Fla., and surrounding Volusia County, and can be enjoyed at every pizzeria and corner diner in the area. The thin shreds of ham, which often are accompanied by mild salami, and a proliferation of crumbled feta cheese set this salad apart. This Greek salad can serve as the centerpiece of a light summer meal or as a side dish to takeout pizza, grilled chicken or steaks.

For the dressing:
$1/_4$ cup olive oil
2 tablespoons red wine vinegar
$1/_2$ teaspoon garlic salt
$1/_4$ teaspoon freshly ground black pepper
$1/_4$ teaspoon sugar

For the salad:
1 8-ounce bag iceberg shreds
$1/_4$ pound sliced boiled ham,
 cut into matchstick strips
$1/_2$ tomato, thinly sliced
$1/_2$ medium onion, thinly sliced, optional
12 Calamata olives
8 pepperoncini peppers
2 ounces crumbled regular
 or reduced-fat feta cheese
$1/_2$ teaspoon dried oregano

Combine dressing ingredients in a small jar and shake well to combine.

Layer salad ingredients in order listed.
Pour dressing over salad and toss before dividing onto 4 dinner plates.

Makes 2 main dish or 4 side dish servings.

Quick Tip: How to handle fresh herbs

Fresh herbs are highly perishable, so buy only what you will use over a few days. Some suggest placing the cut ends of the herbs in a glass of water prior to refrigerating, but I've only had marginal luck with this procedure. No matter what, fresh herbs are going to wilt shortly after they're purchased.

When you're ready to use your herbs, gently rinse them with water, and spin them dry with a salad spinner or gingerly blot them with paper towels. Many herbs, like fresh basil, are subject to bruising, so the general rule of thumb is to handle them with care.

Quick Tip: Using fresh basil

Fresh basil is wonderful in everything from this recipe for Chopped Salad, to pesto sauce. Make enough Pesto Sauce to toss with two servings of pasta by combining 1 cup of packed fresh basil leaves (about two packages from the supermarket) with a clove of crushed garlic, a tablespoon or two of pine nuts and $^1/_2$ cup each extra virgin olive oil and freshly grated parmesan cheese in a food processor or blender. Process until smooth, scraping down the sides of the container once or twice.

Basil has a crisp, slightly anise flavor. The leaves are wonderful tossed in with salad greens.

Chopped Salad with Lemon Vinaigrette

Chopped Salad with Lemon Vinaigrette

Chopped salads are a trendy item on restaurant menus at the moment, and I love the texture these salads offer. My version makes use of leftover grilled chicken breasts, but supermarket rotisserie chicken or even Thanksgiving turkey leftovers can be used. This salad is filling enough to serve as a light summer entrée. Just add some good bread and dig in!

Lemon Vinaigrette:
Juice of one lemon
1 tablespoon chopped fresh basil
1 teaspoon Dijon mustard
1 teaspoon Worcestershire sauce
1 teaspoon salt
$^1/_2$ teaspoon freshly ground black pepper
$1^1/_2$ teaspoon minced garlic (2 cloves)

Salad:
1 head Romaine lettuce, cut into thin strands
1 8-ounce package iceberg shreds
1 cup fresh basil leaves, cut into thin strands
2 cups diced leftover grilled chicken, rotisserie chicken
   or roast turkey
4 ounces hard salami, diced
1 cup canned chick peas, rinsed and drained
2 large ripe tomatoes, chopped
4 ounces crumbled feta cheese
2 green onions, chopped

Whisk vinaigrette ingredients together in a small bowl and set aside. Toss Romaine, iceberg and basil leaves together in a large serving bowl. Top with remaining ingredients and toss with the vinaigrette.

Makes 4 dinner-sized salads.

Mixed Greens with Blue Cheese, Sugared Pecans and Balsamic Honey Mustard Dressing

Mixed Greens with Blue Cheese, Sugared Pecans and Balsamic Honey Mustard Dressing

Mixed Greens with Blue Cheese, Sugared Pecans and Balsamic Honey Mustard Dressing

In almost everything, there's a fine line between the "good" and the "great." In this special-occasion salad, bagged mixed greens are topped with sliced fresh mushrooms and green onion, crumbled blue cheese, dried cranberries and sugared pecans. Then they are drizzled with a simple yet luscious balsamic honey mustard dressing. Although it's more work than most of my "quick cooking" recipes, this is a salad that's sure to impress your guests.

For the Salad:

6 cups mixed lettuce greens, washed
    and torn into bite-sized pieces
3 whole mushrooms, sliced
2 green onions, sliced
1 recipe Sugared Pecans*

4 ounces blue cheese, crumbled
1¹/₂ cups dried cranberries (Craisins)
Balsamic Honey Mustard Dressing**

Divide greens among 6 salad plates. Divide remaining ingredients among the salads.
Drizzle each salad with some of the dressing before serving.
Makes 6 salads.

*For the Sugared Pecans:

1 tablespoon butter
1 tablespoon sugar
1 teaspoon Worcestershire sauce

Dash cayenne pepper
1 cup pecan halves

Melt butter in a small skillet over medium heat. Stir in the sugar, Worcestershire and cayenne and bring to a boil.
Reduce heat and stir in pecans. Stir constantly, until sugar is caramelized and pecans are toasted, 3 to 5 minutes.
Pour on a foil-lined baking sheet to cool.
Makes 1 cup.

**Balsamic Honey Mustard Dressing

¹/₂ cup vegetable oil
¹/₃ cup balsamic vinegar
3 tablespoons honey

2 tablespoons Dijon mustard
¹/₂ teaspoon salt
¹/₄ teaspoon freshly ground black pepper

Combine all ingredients in a small bowl or jar and stir or shake to combine. Refrigerate until ready to serve.
Makes 1 cup dressing.

Oriental Peanut Noodles

Few dishes can boast the versatility of being delicious hot, cold or at room temperature. Ratatouille and potato-leek soup (called Vichyssoise when cold) come to mind. But perhaps my favorite all-temperature side dish is Oriental Peanut Noodles.

8 ounces dried linguine or vermicelli
3 green onions, chopped
3 tablespoons rice wine vinegar
3 tablespoons peanut butter
1 tablespoon honey
2 tablespoons soy sauce
2 tablespoons sesame oil
$^1/_4$ teaspoon Tabasco
$^1/_4$ teaspoon red pepper flakes, optional
$^1/_3$ cup orange juice

Oriental Peanut Noodles

Cook the pasta according to package directions. Combine remaining ingredients in a small bowl. Drain pasta, and toss with the dressing. Serve hot, cold or at room temperature.

Makes 4 to 6 servings.

Quick Tips:

Oriental Peanut Noodles pair wonderfully with many grilled entrees. At my house, this luscious combination is served first as a warm side dish with grilled, teriyaki-marinated chicken breasts or tuna steaks. Steamed sugar snap or snow peas are the perfect vegetable accompaniment.

When dinner is over, I dice up the leftover chicken or tuna and toss with the remaining noodles and peas for a delicious Oriental pasta salad later.

My Chicken Salad

Making wonderful chicken salad is a Southern tradition. I've sampled the best, and here's my version – with a kick of tarragon and a hint of chopped pecans. Serve with buttery rectangular crackers at a luncheon or as hors d'oeuvres. Or, bake in a pie shell for my Chicken Salad Pie (see page 59).

2 cups cooked and cubed chicken breast meat
Salt and freshly ground black pepper
$^1/_2$ cup chopped pecans
2 stalks celery, chopped (about $^3/_4$ cup)

$^1/_2$ teaspoon dried tarragon
$^1/_2$ cup reduced-fat mayonnaise
$^1/_2$ cup reduced-fat sour cream

Place chicken chunks in a bowl and season to taste with salt and pepper. Add remaining ingredients and toss. Refrigerate until ready to serve.

Makes 3 cups chicken salad.

Mandarin Coleslaw

My Mandarin Slaw is a snap to toss together. In fact, you can whip up a batch in minutes with a bag of shredded cabbage for coleslaw from the produce department, a container of vanilla yogurt from the dairy case and a can of mandarin oranges from the canned fruit aisle. Rice wine vinegar gives the dressing a tangy kick, and celery seed adds great flavor. I like to serve this delicious slaw at fish fries and summer cookouts.

Mandarin Coleslaw

1 bag shredded cabbage for coleslaw
1 11-ounce can mandarin oranges, drained,
   2 tablespoons of the juices reserved
1 cup lowfat vanilla yogurt

2 tablespoons rice wine or cider vinegar
$^{1}/_{2}$ teaspoon celery seed
$^{1}/_{4}$ teaspoon freshly ground black pepper
Salt to taste

Place the shredded cabbage in a large bowl. Top with the mandarin oranges.

Combine the yogurt, 2 tablespoons of the reserved juice from the oranges, vinegar, celery seed, black pepper and salt to taste in a bowl. Toss with the cabbage and oranges. Cover and refrigerate until well chilled.

Makes 6 servings.

Warm Asparagus Salad with Country Ham Vinaigrette

I'm always on the lookout for new ways to serve asparagus. I've grilled it, oven-roasted it, and of course, I've steamed it. My recipe for Warm Asparagus Salad takes your standard steamed asparagus to new heights as a first course with a Southern twist – a drizzle of warm Country Ham Vinaigrette. It's the perfect first course when entertaining!

Warm Asparagus Salad With Country Ham Vinaigrette

 1 bunch asparagus, washed and trimmed
$^{1}/_{3}$ cup olive oil
4 ounces finely diced country ham or smoked ham
$^{1}/_{2}$ cup cider vinegar

2 tablespoons bacon drippings, optional
1 tablespoon Dijon mustard
$^{1}/_{2}$ teaspoon salt
$^{1}/_{2}$ teaspoon freshly ground black pepper

Bring 1-inch of water to a boil in a saucepan fitted with a steamer. Add the asparagus, cover with a tight-fitting lid and steam for 3 minutes, until barely crisp-tender. Remove and set aside.

Heat the olive oil in a sauté pan over medium-high heat. Add the ham and cook until golden brown. Stir in the remaining ingredients and bring to a simmer.

Divide the asparagus among 4 salad plates and drizzle with the vinaigrette.

Makes 4 first-course servings.

Tomato-Herb Salad

If you're new to using fresh herbs, my Tomato-Herb Salad is a great place to start. It combines ripe tomatoes with fresh basil and mint for a light and luscious taste of summer. Just be sure to save this recipe for when summer tomatoes are at their peak – late July through September. Then find the best tomatoes you can get your hands on. Look for fresh mozzarella packed in water in plastic containers in the specialty cheese section of most supermarkets.

4 large vine-ripened tomatoes, cored
   and cut into chunks
8 ounces fresh mozzarella,
   drained and cut into cubes
$^1/_3$ cup packed fresh basil leaves,
   washed and dried well (about 10 leaves)
2 tablespoons packed fresh mint leaves,
   washed and dried well (about 12 leaves)
3 tablespoons olive oil
   (preferably extra virgin)
2 tablespoons red wine or sherry vinegar
Salt and freshly ground black pepper,
   to taste

Tomato-Herb Salad

Place the tomato and mozzarella cubes in a bowl. Tear the herbs into small pieces and add to the bowl. Drizzle with the olive oil and vinegar, season with salt and black pepper and toss gently.

Makes 4 servings.

Quick Tip:
A small salad spinner is perfect for washing and drying fresh herbs. If you don't have a spinner, rinse the herbs under running water and pat dry between paper towels.

Quick Tip: How to use fresh herbs

When cooking with fresh herbs, there are a few important things to remember. First, fresh herbs are best added at the end of cooking time. If you wish to use fresh oregano and basil in place of dried in your favorite marinara, add them just before serving for the most flavor.

I often will cook with both forms of herbs, adding some dried herbs in the beginning of a recipe, and finishing the dish with some fresh herbs to add another level of flavor.

You'll usually need three times more fresh herbs than dried when substituting them in recipes. If your recipe calls for 1 teaspoon of a dried herb, in general you'll need 1 tablespoon of fresh. I've found, however, that fresh rosemary and thyme can be used at about the same measurements as their dried counterparts.

4

Bagged Chicken and Tortellini Alfredo

poultry

Bagged Chicken and Tortellini Alfredo

Cooking in a baking bag is something I usually limit to pot roasts and whole chickens. However, after seeing the ingenious ways baking bags were used at the Southern Living Cooking School several years ago, I decided to come up with a recipe of my own. Here, you simply toss together a jar of pasta sauce, frozen tortellini, fresh chicken and some fresh vegetables, then bake.

1 large Reynolds baking bag
1 tablespoon all-purpose flour
1 16-ounce jar regular or reduced-fat
  creamy Parmesan or Alfredo sauce
1 14.5-ounce can reduced-sodium chicken broth
1 19-ounce bag frozen meat-filled tortellini
1 pound boneless, skinless chicken breast halves, sliced
8 ounces sliced fresh mushrooms
$^1/_2$ red bell pepper, sliced
$^1/_2$ teaspoon garlic powder
$^1/_4$ teaspoon freshly ground black pepper
Grated Parmesan cheese, for garnish

Preheat oven to 350 degrees.

Place the flour in the bag and shake well. Add sauce and chicken broth and stir or squeeze to combine. Add remaining ingredients, coating well with the liquids and squeezing to combine. Twist the top of the bag and seal with the enclosed twist-tie. Place on a baking dish and puncture several holes in bag. Bake for 45 minutes. Allow to sit for 5 minutes before serving. Pour onto a large serving platter, sprinkle with the Parmesan cheese and serve.

Makes 6 servings.

Serve with: Store-prepared or refrigerated ready-to-bake garlic breadsticks and mixed greens tossed with diced tomato, cucumber and bottled vinaigrette. For dessert, sprinkle fresh or canned pineapple slices with brown sugar and broil until the sugar is bubbly. Serve with vanilla ice cream or frozen yogurt.

Cheryl's Greek Chicken

My friend Cheryl Steele shared this speedy, yet elegant chicken entrée. It's become a favorite of many friends and readers because it's easy to prepare and good enough for company. Another friend, Rebecca Rule, has made this her signature dish, serving the chicken and pan juices over linguine.

4 boneless, skinless chicken breast halves
1 tablespoon olive oil
1 teaspoon minced garlic (1 large clove)
$^1/_2$ teaspoon dried oregano
1 3.5-ounce package crumbled regular or reduced-fat feta cheese
$^1/_2$ cup freshly squeezed lemon juice (the juice from approximately 3 lemons)

Cheryl's Greek Chicken

Preheat oven to 350 degrees.

Place chicken breasts on a plate. Combine the olive oil and garlic in a small bowl and drizzle over the chicken breasts. Rub the oil mixture into each breast and place in a glass baking dish. Sprinkle the oregano evenly over each breast, then follow with the crumbled feta cheese. Pour the lemon juice over the chicken and bake for 40 minutes.

Makes 4 servings.

Serve with: Mixed greens with strawberries, mushrooms, sliced green onions and prepared poppy seed dressing and cooked white rice or linguine. For dessert, slice some store-bought pound cake, top with butter pecan ice cream and drizzle with warm caramel topping.

BBQ Chicken Pizza

BBQ Chicken Pizza

"Chicken on pizza?" you might ask. In fact, chicken pizza has been a big trend for almost 10 years now, beginning at The California Pizza Kitchen chain and recently trickling down to pizza delivery chains. Preparing your gourmet chicken pizza at home couldn't be simpler. All you need is a prepared pizza crust, bottled barbecue sauce, shredded mozzarella cheese, cooked chicken and sliced red onion. Voila!

1 10-ounce pre-baked pizza shell, such as Boboli
$1/2$ cup prepared barbecue sauce, divided
1 9-ounce package frozen cooked chicken breast strips, thawed*
1 cup shredded part-skim mozzarella cheese
$1/2$ small red onion, sliced
Chopped fresh cilantro or Italian parsley, for garnish

Preheat oven to 400 degrees.

Place pizza shell on a pizza stone or baking sheet. Spread $1/4$ cup of the barbecue sauce over the shell. Combine remaining sauce with chicken strips in a medium bowl. Sprinkle all but $1/4$ cup of the cheese over the barbecue sauce. Top with the chicken and red onion and sprinkle with the remaining cheese. Bake 10 to 15 minutes, until cheese is melted and pizza heated through. Sprinkle with chopped cilantro or parsley. Cut into 8 wedges and serve.

Makes 4 servings.

*Substitute 2 raw boneless, skinless chicken breast halves for the chicken strips, and sauté them in a bit of olive oil in a hot skillet until cooked through.

Serve with: Fresh fruit salad and Italian ice pops for dessert.

Quick Tip:

Think beyond barbecue and tomato sauce to come up with your own chicken pizza variations. Thai peanut sauce, Caribbean jerk sauce, Alfredo sauce and pesto are all good flavor bases. Then, customize your pizza by adding sliced red bell peppers, mushrooms and other toppings which compliment the sauce.

One-Pot Chicken Lo Mien

One-Pot Chicken Lo Mien

Takeout food is part of our busy times, and Chinese takeout is a family favorite. But you can prepare a great Chinese-inspired meal at home with a few ingredients and a lot less fat. Lo Mien is one of my favorite Chinese takeout items, so I came up with a way to create a great, quick lo mien at home while dirtying up just one large skillet.

1 tablespoon dark sesame oil
³/₄ pound chicken tenderloin pieces,
   cut in half lengthwise
3 cups reduced-sodium chicken broth
¹/₂ teaspoon dried ginger
¹/₄ teaspoon dried red pepper flakes
   (or less, to taste)
¹/₄ cup teriyaki sauce
1 9-ounce package refrigerated linguine
1 16-ounce package frozen broccoli,
   carrots and water chestnuts
3 green onions, sliced on the diagonal

Heat the oil in a large skillet over medium-high heat. Add the chicken pieces and sauté until golden brown and cooked through. Remove from the skillet and set aside.

Add the chicken broth, ginger, red pepper flakes and teriyaki sauce to the skillet and bring to a boil. Add the linguine and cook until the pasta is almost done, about 3 minutes. Add the frozen vegetables and return to a boil. Add the reserved chicken and the green onions, and simmer until the vegetables are tender-crisp and the pasta is done.

Makes 6 servings.

Serve with: This dish is a complete, one-skillet meal. You could begin your meal with a fruit salad, then finish with a dessert of fortune cookies and ice cream.

Chicken Provençal

Looking for a way to enjoy summer's abundant produce? My Chicken Provençal is a light, delicious and healthy way to serve chicken with loads of fresh vegetables.

3 boneless, skinless chicken breast halves,
   sliced in half horizontally into 6 cutlets
1 tablespoon olive oil
1 small onion, peeled and diced (about ¹/₂ cup)
2 small zucchini, washed and diced
2 yellow squash, washed and diced
1 14.5-ounce can diced tomatoes seasoned with basil,
   garlic and oregano, undrained
Salt and freshly ground black pepper to taste

Spray a large nonstick skillet with cooking spray and heat over medium-high. Add the chicken pieces and brown, about 3 minutes per side. (Work in batches so that the chicken pieces do not overlap.) Repeat with remaining chicken pieces. Remove from skillet and set aside.

Place pan over medium-high heat and add the olive oil. Add onion and sauté 3 minutes. Add the zucchini and yellow squash and sauté 3 minutes more. Add the tomatoes and return the chicken pieces to the skillet. Bring to a boil, and then reduce heat and simmer, covered, for 10 minutes.

Chicken Provençal

Makes 6 servings.

Serve with: Cooked white rice or pasta. For dessert, combine a half-pint of washed fresh blueberries with a bottle of blueberry fruit syrup in a medium saucepan and bring to a boil. Set aside to cool, and then pour over lemon sorbet or vanilla ice cream.

Chicken Normandy

Chicken Normandy

Apples are abundant in the fall, but instead of baking them into a pie, how about adding them to a delicious entrée – Chicken Normandy. Normandy, France, is known for its apples, so this traditional French dish bears the name of the town. My version is extra easy and is the perfect centerpiece of an autumn meal.

4 boneless, skinless chicken breast halves, sliced in half horizontally into 8 cutlets
$^1/_2$ cup all-purpose flour
$^1/_2$ teaspoon salt
Freshly ground black pepper, to taste

$^1/_2$ cup thinly sliced onion
1 Granny Smith apple, peeled, cored and thinly sliced
1 cup apple cider or juice
$^1/_2$ cup whipping cream
Salt, to taste

Place flour, $^1/_2$ teaspoon salt and pepper to taste on a dinner plate and stir to combine. Dredge both sides of each chicken cutlet in the seasoned flour.

Spray a large nonstick skillet with cooking spray. Heat the skillet at medium-high and add 4 of the chicken cutlets. Brown 2 to 3 minutes, then turn to brown on other side. Remove to a plate and set aside. Continue until all chicken cutlets are browned.

Add the onions to the skillet and sauté until wilted and translucent, about 3 minutes. Add the apple slices and sauté 2 to 3 minutes more, until they begin to soften. Pour in the apple cider and whipping cream and bring to a boil. Return the chicken cutlets to the skillet, reduce heat and simmer until sauce is reduced slightly and chicken is done, about 5 minutes more. Taste the sauce for seasonings, and add salt and pepper, if needed, to taste.

Makes 8 servings.

Serve with: Egg noodles and steamed zucchini slices, green beans or broccoli. For dessert, pick up a custard or almond tart from your favorite bakery or supermarket.

Chicken Taco Rice

Packaged convenience dinners abound in supermarkets today. From ready-to-sauté bags in the freezer section to boxed meal starters, they make getting dinner on the table quick and easy. While these products are convenient, they can be pricey as well as skimpy in servings. There's really no need to spend big bucks on convenience dinners when you can have a one-skillet, child-pleasing meal on the table in 30 minutes or less.

1 tablespoon vegetable oil
1 pound boneless, skinless chicken breast halves, sliced into $^1/_2$-inch strips
1 small onion, chopped (about $^3/_4$ cup)
$1^1/_2$ cups water
1 8-ounce can tomato sauce
1 package taco seasoning mix
1 14.5-ounce can Mexicali corn, drained
1 4-ounce can diced green chiles
$1^1/_2$ cups instant or Minute rice
1 tablespoon chopped fresh parsley, for garnish
$^1/_2$ cup shredded cheddar cheese, for garnish

Chicken Taco Rice

Heat the oil in a large skillet over medium-high heat. Add the chicken and onions, and sauté until lightly browned. Add water, tomato sauce and taco seasoning mix. Bring to a boil. Reduce heat, cover and simmer 5 minutes. Add corn and green chiles and bring to a boil. Stir in the rice, cover and remove from heat. Let stand 5 minutes, or until rice is tender. Fluff with a fork and sprinkle with the chopped parsley and shredded cheese.

Makes 6 servings.

Serve with: Mixed greens topped with a can of drained mandarin oranges, sliced avocado and red onions tossed with creamy Italian dressing. For dessert, pick up some lime sherbet from the supermarket and top with sliced strawberries or pineapple chunks.

Chicken Florentine

My Chicken Florentine is the answer to your "what to do with chicken" dilemma, and is a cinch to prepare. The secret: Frozen creamed spinach. The delicious spinach sauce will impress your guests, and no one needs to know it came from a package.

3 boneless, skinless chicken breast halves
   sliced in half horizontally into 6 cutlets
2 tablespoons all-purpose flour
Salt and freshly ground black pepper, to taste
1 tablespoon olive oil
1 tablespoon butter or margarine
2 9-ounce packages frozen creamed spinach, defrosted
$^1/_2$ cup shredded Swiss cheese, divided
$^1/_4$ teaspoon nutmeg

Chicken Florentine

Preheat oven to 350 degrees.

Place the flour on a plate and season with salt and pepper. Heat the oil and butter in a large skillet over medium-high heat. Dredge the chicken pieces in the seasoned flour and add to the hot skillet. Brown on both sides (about 3 minutes per side). Work in batches so that the chicken pieces do not overlap. Repeat with remaining chicken pieces. Set aside.

Combine creamed spinach in a bowl with half of the shredded cheese and the nutmeg. Spread half of the spinach mixture in the bottom of a 9-by-13-inch glass baking dish that has been sprayed with non-stick cooking spray. Place the browned chicken pieces over the spinach and spread the remaining spinach mixture over the chicken pieces. Sprinkle with the remaining cheese and bake, uncovered, for 25 minutes.

Makes 6 servings.

Serve with: Mixed greens tossed with mandarin orange segments, sliced black olives, chopped green onions and sweet and sour dressing, and cooked white rice. For dessert, try some strawberry sorbet drizzled with warm caramel sauce.

Quick Tip:

Instead of pounding and pounding and pounding boneless chicken breast halves into a nice uniform thickness, I often slice them in half horizontally. Chicken breasts these days are often huge, so besides saving your "pounding arm," you're also cutting back on your serving size without much effort. Slicing the chicken breast in half is easy once you get the hang of it. Simply place a breast half on a flat work surface, then use a long serrated knife to slice the breast into two cutlets. Some supermarkets are beginning to carry chicken cutlets, saving you even more preparation time!

Elegant Chicken Roll-Ups

While this recipe may appear more daunting than most of my "quick cooking" recipes, the preparation can be broken down into steps, and the dish can be prepared in advance. It's a wonderful dinner party entrée, based on a dish called Chicken Saltimboca that appears in "Tea-Time at the Masters." I put my signature on the dish by substituting mixed dried herbs from a jar – rather than measuring out six different dried herbs – and added sundried tomato spread for extra flavor.

Elegant Chicken Roll-Ups

6 boneless, skinless chicken
  breast halves
6 thin slices prosciutto
  (about ¼ pound total)
1 cup shredded mozzarella cheese
6 tablespoons sundried tomato spread
  and sauce

¼ cup (½ stick) butter
  or margarine, melted
  OR 2 egg whites
1 cup dried breadcrumbs
½ cup shredded Parmesan cheese
1 teaspoon Italian seasoning

Preheat oven to 350 degrees.

Pound chicken breasts between heavy duty plastic wrap with flat side of a meat mallet to an even ¼-inch thickness. Lay a piece of prosciutto on each chicken breast then spread with 1 tablespoon of the tomato spread. Sprinkle with a bit of the mozzarella cheese, then roll up and secure with strong toothpicks.

Combine breadcrumbs, Parmesan cheese and Italian seasoning in a pie plate or shallow baking dish. Dip each chicken breast in the melted butter, coating well on all sides. Then, dip into the breadcrumb mixture. Place on a baking sheet and repeat until all chicken is coated. *

Bake chicken roll-ups 35 minutes, until cooked through.
Remove toothpicks before serving.

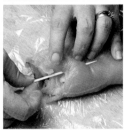

Makes 6 servings.

Serve with: Cooked fettuccine tossed with purchased Alfredo sauce, bagged salad greens with tomato slices and Caesar or creamy Italian dressing. Pick up a New York style cheesecake from the bakery or frozen desserts section of your supermarket, cut into slices and drizzle with strawberry ice cream topping.

*The completed chicken rolls can be refrigerated, tightly covered, overnight. Alternately, they can be frozen for up to a month. However, be sure that you use fresh, not previously frozen chicken breast halves. You should not freeze raw chicken that was previously frozen.

Quick Tip:

Vary the fillings for these versatile chicken roll-ups. Spread the chicken breasts with herbed cheese spread, add some good sliced ham and a spear or two of fresh asparagus before rolling. Or, substitute prepared pesto sauce for the sundried tomato spread.

Cornbread-Topped Chicken Casserole

This is a hearty main dish with a Southern accent. What starts out as your usual chicken casserole gets a new twist with a topping of crumbled cornbread.

3 tablespoon butter or margarine, divided
$^1/_4$ cup chopped onion ($^1/_2$ small onion)
$^1/_4$ cup chopped celery (1 rib celery)
$2^1/_2$ cups cooked and cubed chicken
1 $10^3/_4$-ounce can Healthy Request
  Cream of Chicken Soup
$^1/_2$ cup skim milk
1 2-ounce jar diced pimentos
1 10-ounce package frozen peas and carrots, defrosted
1 8.5-ounce box Jiffy Corn Muffin Mix,
  prepared and baked according to package directions

Preheat oven to 350 degrees.

Heat 1 tablespoon of the butter or margarine in a skillet. Add the onion and celery and sauté until tender and translucent. Remove from the heat and stir in the chicken, cream of chicken soup, milk, pimientos, peas and carrots. Pour into a 9-by-13 inch glass baking dish. Crumble the prepared corn muffins over the top. Melt the remaining 2 tablespoons butter or margarine and drizzle over the top. Bake for 30 to 40 minutes, until the crumbs are lightly browned and the casserole is bubbly.

Makes 6 servings.

Serve with: Sliced tomatoes. For dessert, pick up a cream pie from your supermarket's bakery section.

Quick Tip:

Some supermarkets carry cornbread or corn muffins in the bakery department, and rounds of cornbread in the freezer section.

Cornbread-Topped Chicken Casserole

Hot Turkey Salad

This is the turkey, celery, mayonnaise and cheese casserole topped with crushed potato chips that so often appeared at church suppers and ladies luncheons way back when. The combination still satisfies, and makes wonderful use of leftover turkey or chicken.

3 cups cooked, diced turkey
  or chicken
Salt and freshly ground black pepper,
  to taste
2 cups chopped celery (about 4 ribs)
$^1/_2$ cup slivered almonds

1 cup reduced-fat mayonnaise
$^1/_2$ cup shredded cheddar cheese
1 cup crushed potato chips
  (4 cups of potato chips make 1 cup
  crushed)

Preheat oven to 350 degrees.

Place diced turkey in a medium bowl and season to taste with salt and pepper. Add the celery, almonds, mayonnaise and cheese and stir well to combine. Spread the turkey salad in a 9-by-9-inch glass baking dish that has been sprayed with nonstick cooking spray and top with the crushed potato chips. Bake for 20 to 30 minutes, until hot and bubbly.

Makes 6 servings.

Serve with: Warm dinner rolls and cooked green peas. For dessert, drizzle some raspberry syrup over peach ice cream for Peach Melba sundaes.

Creamy Chicken and Spinach Lasagna

Creamy Chicken and Spinach Lasagna

Lasagna's lengthy preparation – boiling noodles, simmering a sauce and putting it all together – used to take it out of the "quick cooking realm". That was until I came up with this recipe for Creamy Chicken and Spinach Lasagna. I developed the recipe to prove that you could prepare an elegant and delicious lasagna without much preparation time. And, I wanted to come up with an alternative to the traditional lasagna combination of noodles, cheeses and meat sauce. The resulting dish is a delicious departure from traditional lasagna. Don't let the long list of ingredients intimidate you – I promise there's absolutely no cooking involved until you pop the lasagna into the oven!

Spinach layer:
2 10-ounce packages frozen chopped spinach, thawed and squeezed of excess liquid
15 ounces fat-free cottage cheese
1 large egg
1 teaspoon Italian seasoning
$1/2$ teaspoon garlic salt
$1/4$ teaspoon freshly ground black pepper
Dash nutmeg
Dash cayenne

Combine all ingredients in a medium bowl and set aside.

Chicken layer:
3 cups cooked, cubed chicken
2 green onions, finely chopped
2 $10^3/4$-ounce cans Healthy Request Cream of Chicken Soup
1 cup reduced-fat sour cream
$1/2$ cup shredded Parmesan cheese
$1/4$ teaspoon freshly ground black pepper

Combine all ingredients in a medium bowl and set aside.

Other ingredients:
1 28-ounce or 2 14.5-ounce cans diced tomatoes seasoned with basil, garlic and oregano, undrained
2 cups shredded Italian-style 6-cheese blend or shredded part-skim Mozzarella cheese
12 uncooked no-boil lasagna noodles

Assembly:
Preheat oven to 350 degrees.

Spray a 9-by-13-inch glass baking dish with nonstick cooking spray.

Spread a heaping $1/2$ cup of the diced tomatoes (with juice) on the bottom of the prepared baking dish. Top with 4 noodles. Spread with $1/2$ of the spinach mixture, $1/2$ of the chicken mixture and $1/2$ cup of the shredded cheese.

Top with 4 more noodles. Spread with $1/2$ cup of the diced tomatoes, the remaining spinach, the remaining chicken and $1/2$ cup of the cheese.

Top with 4 more noodles. Spread with the remaining diced tomatoes and juices. (Refrigerate the remaining cheese.) Cover tightly with aluminum foil* and bake for 50 minutes. Remove from oven, remove foil and sprinkle with remaining cheese. Return to oven for 5 minutes more, until cheese is melted. Let stand 10 minutes before serving.

Makes 8-12 servings.

*I tested the recipe to determine its make-ahead potential, and fully assembled it 24 hours before baking. It came out perfect after spending the night in the refrigerator, tightly covered with foil. I simply let it sit at room temperature for 30 minutes before baking.

Serve with: Bakery rolls and a tossed salad. For dessert, pick up a carton of peppermint ice cream and top it with hot fudge sauce.

Rotisserie Chicken Hero

This Rotisserie Chicken Hero starts with a store-roasted chicken that you can pick up at most any supermarket. Layered on challah (egg bread), along with lettuce, tomato, avocado, bacon, sliced cheddar cheese and Thousand Island dressing, it's the perfect after-church lunch or weekend picnic fare. Use the recipe as a guide, deleting or adding ingredients according to your family's preferences.

1 loaf challah bread, French bread or other
   oval or round loaf
$1/2$ cup prepared Thousand Island dressing
1 whole rotisserie chicken
6 large lettuce leaves, washed and dried
1 large tomato, sliced
Salt and freshly ground black pepper, to taste
1 avocado, seed removed, peeled and sliced
8 strips bacon, cooked and drained
Sliced cheddar cheese

Rotisserie Chicken Hero

Slice the loaf of bread in half horizontally. Spread both cut sides of the loaf with the dressing. Set aside.

Remove the skin from the chicken and discard. Remove the chicken meat from the bones and shred. Set aside.

Place the lettuce leaves and tomato slices evenly over the bottom bread half. Season the tomatoes with salt and pepper, to taste. Mound the chicken over the tomatoes. Place the avocado slices over the chicken, then top with the strips of bacon and cheddar cheese. Place the top half of the bread over the cheese. Slice into 6 sandwiches and serve.

Makes 6 servings.

Hot Chicken Subs

Hot Chicken Subs

Hot Chicken Subs are a "supper-worthy" sandwich. You see, there's a difference between a "lunch sandwich" and a sandwich supper. And the difference is in the attention paid to each element, versus the assembly-line slapping together of sandwich ingredients. Here, boneless, skinless chicken breast halves get a flavor boost from a prepared marinade, then are layered with sharp cheddar cheese and served on toasted rolls.

4 boneless, skinless chicken
   breast halves
4 teaspoons Dale's Marinade*
4 6-inch French rolls
2 tablespoons melted butter
   or margarine, optional

4 slices cheddar cheese
2 tablespoons reduced-fat
   mayonnaise

Place the chicken and the Dale's Marinade in a gallon zip-top plastic bag. Squeeze to coat the chicken pieces with the marinade. Refrigerate for 30 minutes.

Place a large skillet over medium to medium-high heat. When hot, add the chicken breasts. (Discard marinade and bag.) Cook the chicken breasts on one side for 4 minutes, without moving. Turn and cook on other side 4 minutes. Turn again, cover and cook 5 minutes more, until cooked through. (Internal temperature when checked with an instant-read meat thermometer should be 170 degrees.)

Meanwhile, split the rolls in half and brush with the melted butter. Toast or broil until lightly browned. Spread with the mayonnaise, and top with a chicken breast, slices of cheese and the roll top. Slice in half and serve.

Makes 4 servings.

* Dale's Marinade can be found in most Southeastern supermarkets in the condiment aisle, near the steak and barbecue sauces.

Slow Cooker Chicken and Dumplings

There's nothing quite as satisfying as chicken and dumplings, but who has the time to prepare it? If you've got the craving – and a slow cooker – here's the recipe for you.

1 3¹/₂-pound chicken, skinned
2 carrots, peeled and sliced diagonally
  into 1-inch pieces
1 small onion, chopped
2 stalks celery, washed and coarsely chopped
2 bay leaves

1 teaspoon salt
2 teaspoons dried parsley flakes
¹/₂ teaspoon poultry seasoning
Freshly ground black pepper, to taste
2 quarts water
1 12-ounce package frozen dumplings*

Place the chicken in the ceramic vessel of a 4 to 5-quart slow cooker. Sprinkle the carrots, onion and celery over the chicken. Add the bay leaves, and sprinkle in the salt, parsley, poultry seasoning and black pepper. Pour in the water, cover and turn the slow cooker on to the low setting. Cook 6 to 8 hours, until chicken is tender.

Remove the chicken from the slow cooker and set aside to cool. Strain the broth and remove the carrots. Return the broth to the slow cooker, set the carrots aside and discard the other vegetables. Cover the slow cooker and turn it on to the high setting and bring to a simmer. Add the dumplings, cover and cook 20 to 30 minutes, until tender.

Shred the chicken and return it to the slow cooker, along with the carrots, 10 minutes before serving, to heat through.

Makes 8 servings.

*Frozen dumpling sheets can be found in the frozen foods section of most supermarkets. Most often they will be located near the frozen pastas and bread dough. Two cups of dried wide egg noodles can be substituted.

Serve with: Mixed greens, grape tomatoes and creamy ranch dressing. For dessert, toast prepared pound cake slices in the toaster oven and top with vanilla ice cream and hot fudge sauce.

Slow Cooker Chicken and Dumplings

Quick Tip:

Poultry sheers are a handy gadget to help you get the chicken skinned fast, and the skinless chicken will release less fat into your broth, saving time skimming your broth later on. (Skinning chicken wings is tricky, so I usually don't bother.) For a quicker route, use skinless bone-in chicken breast halves or boneless, skinless chicken breast halves.

Orange Chicken with Fruit Salsa

My mother used to prepare Baked Orange Chicken, in which bone-in chicken pieces were baked in orange soda. I remember loving the dish as a child, but Mom lost the recipe. So, I used the idea as a springboard to this updated, delicious dish of orange-soda marinated chicken and a wonderful fruit salsa. The fruit salsa is also delicious served with tortilla chips!

Orange Chicken with Fruit Salsa

Chicken Marinade:
1 cup orange soda
¼ cup soy sauce
1 teaspoon minced garlic (1 large clove)
½ teaspoon ground ginger
4 boneless, skinless chicken breast halves

Fruit Salsa:
1 tablespoon honey
Juice of 1 lime
½ teaspoon minced garlic (1 medium clove)
1 11-ounce can mandarin oranges, drained
1 11-ounce can pineapple tidbits
  or crushed pineapple, drained
1 kiwi, peeled and diced
1 small red onion, peeled and diced
1 medium jalapeño, seeded and finely chopped
⅓ cup packed fresh basil leaves, chopped

Combine orange soda, soy sauce, minced garlic and ginger in a zip-top plastic bag. Squeeze to combine, and then add the chicken breasts. Refrigerate for several hours or overnight.

Combine the honey, lime juice and minced garlic in a medium bowl. Add the oranges, pineapple, kiwi, onion, jalapeño and basil and stir.
Cover and refrigerate until ready to use.

Preheat a charcoal or gas grill. Remove chicken breasts from marinade and grill 7 minutes per side, or until internal temperature reaches 170 degrees. Serve the chicken immediately, topped with the fruit salsa.

Makes 4 servings.

Serve with: Your favorite chicken-flavored packaged rice mix and steamed broccoli. For dessert, pick up a chocolate cake from the bakery.

Quick Tip:

Use the fruit salsa portion of the recipe as a base to come up with your own fruit salsa. Replace the mandarin oranges with peeled, diced peaches during the summer months when peaches are abundant. The combinations of fruits for this salsa can be endless. Melons of all varieties, especially watermelon, pair well with the spicy onions and peppers and the sweet-tart dressing. Grapes and strawberries also are excellent choices.

Three-Way Sticky, Sweet and Sour Chicken

Three-Way Sticky, Sweet and Sour Chicken

This recipe has been called by many names. From Sweet and Sour Chicken, to Russian and French Chicken, it's been passed around and written up in community cookbooks for years. I call my version Three-Way Sticky, Sweet and Sour Chicken, as the delicious combination of French onion soup mix, preserves and salad dressing create a sticky glaze. Traditionally, this was a preparation for bone-in chicken breast halves, but I have prepared grilled boneless, skinless chicken breast tenderloin fillets and chicken wings using this tasty sauce. The directions for all three are below!

Marinade/sauce:
1 package dry French onion soup mix
1 12-ounce jar all-fruit apricot spread or apricot preserves
1 8-ounce bottle regular, reduced-fat or fat-free French or Russian salad dressing (1 cup)

Combine ingredients in a bowl and set aside.

Chicken: Choose one
6 bone-in, skinless chicken breast halves
2 pounds chicken wings, tips removed and separated at the joint
2 pounds boneless, skinless chicken tenderloin fillets

For chicken breast halves or chicken wings: Preheat oven to 350 degrees. Place chicken breasts in a 9-by-13-inch glass baking dish. Pour sauce over top and bake for 1 hour, basting several times during baking. (If using wings, toss wings with the sauce to coat before baking.)

For chicken tenderloin fillets: Place marinade/sauce in a gallon sized zip-top plastic bag. Add the tenderloin fillets and marinate in the refrigerator several hours or overnight.

Preheat grill according to manufacturers directions. Skewer fillets with bamboo or metal skewers and grill for 4 to 5 minutes per side, basting with additional marinade towards the end of cooking time. Boil any remaining marinade, cool slightly and serve as a dipping sauce.

Each version makes 6 servings.

Mom's Taco Pie

My mother's recipe for Taco Pie is a quick, child-friendly entrée that gives them all the flavors of their favorite tacos in one great meat pie. She passed the recipe along to me a few years back, and I've developed a version with a fraction of the fat in the original by using reduced-fat sour cream, baked tortilla chips and substituting lean ground turkey for ground beef.

1 pound extra lean ground turkey
2 tablespoons taco seasoning mix
2 tablespoons cold water
8 ounces reduced-fat sour cream
2 tablespoons salsa
2 ounces chopped black olives ($^1/_2$ a 4.25-ounce can)
$^3/_4$ cup coarsely crushed baked tortilla chips
$^1/_2$ cup shredded sharp cheddar cheese

Preheat oven to 375 degrees. Combine turkey, seasonings and water and press in the bottom and up the sides of a 9-inch pie plate. Combine sour cream, salsa, black olives and tortilla chips in a medium bowl and spread over the turkey crust. Sprinkle the cheese over the top and bake for 40 minutes.

Makes 6 servings

Serve with: Packaged Mexican rice and a mixed green salad with diced tomato and cucumber. Toss the salad with your favorite creamy ranch dressing.

Mom's Taco Pie

Bow-Ties with Boursin

Calling a recipe "easy" and "elegant" doesn't have to be an oxymoron. My recipe for Bow-Ties with Boursin illustrates my point perfectly. The clever use of convenience products can add up to full gourmet flavor with a little supermarket savvy. Using stir-fry ready chicken strips, prepared fresh broccoli florets and a carton of herbed cheese spread from the deli department equal a dish that doesn't hint to its ease of preparation!

8 ounces dry bow-tie pasta
2 cups broccoli florets
2 tablespoons butter
  or margarine
$^1/_2$ pound boneless,
  skinless chicken breasts
  halves, cut into thin
  strips or cubed
1 small red bell pepper,
  seeded and cut into thin
  strips
1 cup reduced-sodium
  chicken broth
1 6.5-ounce container
  garlic and herb soft-
  spread cheese*

Bring a large pot of water to a boil over high heat. Add the bow ties and cook according to package directions. Add broccoli florets during last 4 minutes of cooking. Drain and set aside.

Melt the butter or margarine in a large skillet over medium-high heat. Add the chicken and red bell peppers and cook until chicken is done, about 5 minutes. Add the chicken broth and bring to a boil. Reduce heat and stir in the cheese spread. Add the bow ties and broccoli, stirring well to coat with the sauce.

Makes 4 servings.

*A 6.5-ounce container of Allouette garlic and herb cheese was used for testing purposes only. Or, substitute $^1/_2$ cup if the Boursin Cheese Spread on page 15.

Serve with: A green salad tossed with zesty balsamic vinaigrette and some crusty French or Italian bread. Pick up some gourmet ice cream pops for dessert.

Quick Tip:

When serving picky children, omit the broccoli and substitute frozen peas. Place a 10-ounce package of peas in the colander you plan to use to drain the pasta. Drain the pasta over the peas and the hot pasta water will defrost and warm them.

Party-Picnic Chicken

Party-Picnic Chicken

Looking for an effortless entrée for entertaining, or for something elegant to take to the lake for a weekend picnic? Party-Picnic Chicken is cooked up unattended – in your slow cooker, but no one will guess how simple it is to prepare. The flavors of this dish are simply wonderful – you've got salty, sweet, tart and tangy.

1 whole chicken cut up*	2 tablespoons capers
$1/4$ cup orange juice	$1/3$ cup brown sugar
$1/4$ cup olive oil*	$1/3$ cup dried apricots, sliced
$1/4$ cup red wine vinegar	2 bay leaves
$2^1/_2$ teaspoons minced garlic (3 to 4 cloves)	Salt and freshly ground black pepper, to taste
1 tablespoon dried oregano	Chopped fresh parsley, for garnish
$1/3$ cup sliced Spanish green olives	

Arrange the chicken pieces in the ceramic vessel of a slow cooker. Combine the orange juice, olive oil, red wine vinegar, garlic, oregano, green olives and capers in a bowl and pour over the chicken. Sprinkle the brown sugar and apricots over the chicken. Add the bay leaves and season to taste with salt and pepper. Cover and turn slow cooker to low. Cook on low for 6 to 8 hours.

When chicken is tender, remove from the slow cooker and place on a serving platter. Sprinkle with the chopped parsley. Pour the remaining juices into a sauceboat and pass at the table.

Makes 4 servings.

*To decrease the fat in the recipe, remove the skin from all of the chicken pieces except the wings and reduce the olive oil to 1 tablespoon.

Serve with: Couscous Salad and fresh fruit. For dessert, whip up a package of white chocolate pudding and serve with chocolate-filled rolled sugar wafers (tulle cookies).

Quick Tip:

Make a delicious Couscous Salad by combining a box of plain couscous (prepared according to package directions) with $1/2$ cup of golden raisins, 2 chopped green onion, 2 tablespoons of olive oil and $1/3$ cup of orange juice. Season the couscous with salt and pepper to taste, and store in the refrigerator until ready to serve. (You can find packages of couscous near the rice or in the health foods section at your favorite supermarket.)

Chicken Salad Pie

Take my favorite chicken salad, spread it in a pre-baked piecrust and top with shredded Swiss cheese and you've got one great Chicken Salad Pie! This dish is a hit at ladies luncheons or as a light evening meal.

1 piecrust (either refrigerated or frozen),
   pre-baked according to package directions
2 cups cooked and cubed chicken breast meat
Salt and freshly ground black pepper
$^1/_2$ cup chopped pecans
$^3/_4$ cup chopped celery (2 ribs)
$^1/_2$ teaspoon dried tarragon
$^1/_2$ cup reduced-fat mayonnaise
$^1/_2$ cup reduced-fat sour cream
1 cup shredded Swiss cheese, divided

Preheat oven to 350 degrees.

Season the chicken with salt and pepper to taste. Stir in the pecans, celery, tarragon, mayonnaise, sour cream and $^1/_2$ cup of the shredded Swiss cheese. Spread the chicken salad mixture into the prepared piecrust, sprinkle with the remaining Swiss cheese and bake for 25 to 30 minutes.

Makes 8 servings.

Serve with: A fresh fruit salad and bakery blueberry muffins.

Chicken Salad Pie

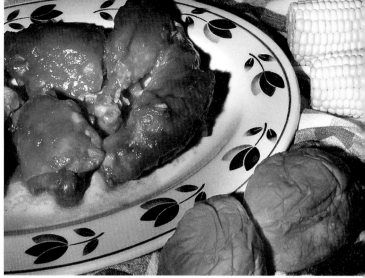
Kids Q

Kids Q

My children love to help out in the kitchen, and my recipe for Kids "Q," based on an old barbecued chicken recipe that called for a combination of ketchup and Coca-Cola, is a recipe they'll enjoy preparing themselves. Traditionally the dish was prepared in the oven, but I've opted to use the slow cooker to keep my kitchen cool. Keep the children safe by eliminating the small onion, which must be chopped, and substitute pre-chopped fresh or frozen onion.

1 package (3 to $3^1/_2$ pounds) "pick of the chix,"
   skin removed*
1 teaspoon barbecue seasoning or seasoning salt, optional
1 small onion, finely chopped (about 1 cup chopped onion)
1 cup ketchup
$^1/_2$ cup Coca-Cola
1 tablespoon Worcestershire sauce

Season both sides of the chicken pieces with the barbecue seasoning and place in vessel of a slow cooker. Combine remaining ingredients in a bowl and pour over the chicken. Cover and cook on low for 6 to 8 hours or on high for 4 hours. Remove the chicken pieces to a serving platter and serve with the remaining sauce on the side.

Makes 4 servings.

*This includes 2 chicken breast halves, 2 thighs and 2 drumsticks.

Serve with: Involve the children in the preparation of the side dishes, too. Children are great at shucking summer's fresh corn, which pairs well with the barbecue chicken. Add some rolls, and give the children lots of praise for a meal they practically prepared all by themselves!

Mother's Chicken and Wild Rice

Chicken and rice casserole was weeknight family food when I was growing up, and consisted of bone-in chicken pieces baked with white rice and cream of mushroom soup. While this was good family fare, my favorite version of chicken and rice casserole was the one my mother served for company. This elaborate recipe involved boiling a whole chicken in water that was flavored with curry powder and sherry, then cooling and shredding the chicken. I've pared the preparation time way down by using leftover rotisserie chicken or turkey, for a delicious casserole to serve to your guests or take to your next covered dish dinner.

3 cups diced cooked chicken or turkey
1 6-ounce package long-grain and
   wild rice mix, cooked according
   to package directions*
1 10^3/$_4$-ounce can Healthy Request
   condensed cream of chicken soup
1 cup reduced-fat sour cream
1 tablespoon dry sherry, optional
^{1}/$_2$ teaspoon curry powder
1 cup sliced almonds, toasted**

Preheat oven to 350 degrees.

Combine chicken pieces and prepared rice mix in a large bowl. In a medium bowl, combine the soup, sour cream, sherry and curry powder. Fold soup mixture into the chicken and rice until well blended. Spread the mixture in a 9-by-13-inch glass baking dish and sprinkle with the almonds. Bake, uncovered, for 1 hour.

Makes 6 to 8 servings.

*Uncle Ben's Original Recipe Long Grain and Wild Rice Mix was used for testing purposes.

**Toast almonds in a skillet over medium-high heat until golden, or in a shallow baking dish in a 350 degree oven for 10 minutes.

Serve with: Steamed green peas and bakery rolls. For dessert, purchase a chocolate or angel food roulade cake from the supermarket bakery, drizzle a bit of raspberry or chocolate sauce on the plate and garnish with fresh berries.

Quick Tip:

An average store-prepared rotisserie chicken will yield approximately 3 cups of shredded or cubed chicken.

Mother's Chicken and Wild Rice

Mom's Party Chicken

When company came for dinner my mother pulled out all the stops, and often served this recipe I call Mom's Party Chicken. This is a nice "company" dish, and it can be assembled a day ahead and refrigerated. Make an assembly line for dredging the chicken with the flour, eggs and breadcrumbs and saute the chicken in batches of four breasts at a time. Mom has often served this entrée for 25 guests or more!

1 cup all-purpose flour
1 teaspoon salt
$^1/_2$ teaspoon freshly ground black pepper
2 eggs, beaten
$1^1/_2$ cups seasoned breadcrumbs
6 boneless, skinless chicken breast halves
2 tablespoons butter
2 tablespoons vegetable oil
8 ounces sliced mushrooms, sauteed in 1 tablespoon butter
   and 1 tablespoon vegetable oil
   or 1 6.5-ounce jar sliced mushrooms, drained,
   liquid reserved
6 ounces sliced mozzarella cheese
$^1/_3$ cup dry white or Marsala wine, sherry or reserved liquid
   from mushrooms

Mom's Party Chicken

Preheat oven to 350 degrees.

Place flour, salt and pepper in a zip-top plastic bag. Place beaten eggs in a pie plate or other shallow dish. Place breadcrumbs in a zip-top plastic bag. Shake one chicken breast at a time in the flour, then dip in the eggs, coating both sides well. Place breast in bag with breadcrumbs and shake well to coat. Repeat with remaining breasts.

Heat butter and oil over medium-high heat until butter is melted. Reduce heat to medium and sauté chicken breasts in two batches, browning well on both sides, about 3 to 5 minutes per side. Place chicken in a 9-by-13-inch glass baking dish. Top each chicken breast with a slice of cheese, then sprinkle the mushrooms over all. Drizzle the wine around the bottom of the baking dish and cover with foil. Bake for 30 minutes.

Makes 6 servings.

Serve with: Steamed baby carrots and your favorite packaged long grain and wild rice mix. Make elegant sundaes of raspberry or strawberry sorbet, dolce de leche ice cream and warm caramel sauce.

5

Rosemary Pork Tenderloin with Balsamic Brown Sauce

beef&pork

Rosemary Pork Tenderloin with Balsamic Brown Sauce

Pork tenderloin is popular not only for its low fat content, but also for its ease of preparation. Here, two tenderloins are rubbed down with crushed garlic and rosemary, then are given a quick searing in a hot skillet. The sauce will make your guests feel like they're dining in a fine restaurant, and your secret will be that the sauce base is a mix! Be sure to use caution when preparing the sauce, since the handle of your skillet will be hot from the oven.

1 1/2 teaspoons minced garlic (2 cloves)
2 tablespoons chopped fresh rosemary
1 package pork tenderloins (2 pieces)
Salt and freshly ground black pepper
1 tablespoon olive oil

2 packages Hunter sauce mix
2 cups water
1/4 cup balsamic vinegar
1 tablespoon butter
1 3.25-ounce jar capers, drained

Preheat oven to 450 degrees.

Combine garlic and chopped rosemary in a small bowl. Rub mixture into the tenderloins and season all over with salt and pepper.

Heat oil in a large skillet with an oven-proof handle over medium heat. Turn every few minutes, until browned on all sides, cooking for about 8 to 10 minutes total. Place skillet in oven and roast 10 to 15 minutes or until internal temperature reaches 150 degrees. Remove skillet from oven, place pork on cutting board and set aside.

Add balsamic vinegar and water to skillet, being careful to use an oven mit before touching the handle of the pan. Whisk in sauce mix and simmer until thickened, about 3 minutes. Whisk in the butter and capers, whisking until the butter is incorporated and the capers heated. Slice pork diagonally into 1/2-inch slices. Drizzle with the sauce and serve.

Makes 6 servings.

C.C.'s Nacho Casserole

My daughter C.C. is a nacho lover, and this recipe for C.C.'s Nacho Casserole gives her the taste of her favorite appetizer in a quick and easy main dish. The recipe is beyond simple, and only calls for four ingredients. You start with a layer of nacho cheese flavored tortilla chips, then pile on seasoned ground beef and shredded cheese. Pop it into the oven, and you've got a child-pleasing main dish.

4 cups Nacho Cheese Doritos
1 pound lean ground beef

1 15-ounce can seasoned diced tomato sauce
    for chili*
2 cups shredded cheddar cheese

Preheat oven to 350 degrees. Spray a 9-by-13-inch glass baking dish with nonstick spray. Spread 3 cups of the Doritos over the bottom of the pan. Crumble the remaining 1 cup of Doritos in a bowl and set aside.

Makes 4 servings.

Brown the ground beef in a large skillet over medium-high heat. Drain well. Return to the skillet. Add the seasoned diced tomato sauce and pour over Doritos. Top with the shredded cheese and remaining crumbled Doritos. Cover with foil and bake for 20 to 30 minutes, until hot and bubbly.

*Hunt's Seasoned Diced Tomato Sauce for Chili was used for testing purposes.

Serve with: Packaged Mexican rice and carrot sticks with Ranch dressing for dipping. Whip up some instant chocolate pudding for dessert.

Beef and Potato Pasties

Beef and Potato Pasties

I enjoyed delicious Cornish Pasties at a sidewalk pasty shop in Reading, England, and came up with a recipe of my own when I returned to the States. Pasties (pronounced like pasta) are savory hand pies filled with potatoes and meat or vegetables. Here, I've combined ground beef, onion, carrots and diced potatoes, then seasoned the mixture with thyme. Defrosted frozen hashbrowns, a can of condensed soup and refrigerated pizza crust dough are the secrets to the speedy preparation of these delicious hand pies.

1 pound lean ground beef
1 small onion, finely chopped
2 small carrots, grated
$^1/_2$ teaspoon thyme
3 cups frozen southern-style hashbrowns, defrosted
   OR peeled and diced fresh potatoes

1 10$^3/_4$-ounce can condensed cream
   of mushroom soup with roasted garlic
Freshly ground black pepper, to taste
2 10-ounce packages refrigerated pizza crust dough
1 egg white

Preheat oven to 400 degrees.

Place ground beef, chopped onion, carrots and thyme in a large skillet. Sauté over medium-high heat, stirring often, for 5 minutes. Add the potatoes and cook 10 to 15 minutes, until potatoes are tender. Remove from heat, stir in the soup and season with black pepper to taste.

Open refrigerated pizza crust dough and cut each roll of dough into 4 equal portions. Roll each piece of dough into an 8-inch circle, and then top with $^1/_2$ cup of the beef and potato filling. Brush the edges of the dough with the egg white, then pinch to seal tightly. Place on a baking sheet and repeat with remaining dough and filling.

Brush outside of each pastry with remaining egg white and bake for 10 minutes.
Reduce heat to 350 degrees and bake an additional 20 minutes, until golden brown.

Makes 8 servings.

Meatball Stroganoff

Frozen meatballs are a super shortcut product for busy cooks. When allowed to simmer all day in the slow cooker with other ingredients, it becomes hard to tell they're not homemade. Here, they become a delicious Meatball Stroganoff that's perfect for weekday family fare.

1 $10^3/_4$-ounce can Healthy Request cream of mushroom soup
1 14.5-ounce can reduced-sodium beef broth
1 18-ounce package frozen fully-cooked meatballs (about 35 meatballs)
8 ounces sliced fresh mushrooms, optional
1 cup reduced-fat sour cream
1 tablespoon all-purpose flour
$^1/_3$ cup water

Meatball Stroganoff

Combine soup and beef broth in a crock pot. Add meatballs and mushrooms, cover and cook on low for 6 to 8 hours.

Combine sour cream, flour and water in a bowl. Stir mixture into meatballs, cover and cook on low for 10 minutes before serving, to thicken sauce.

Makes 6 servings.

Serve with: Cooked egg noodles or white rice and a side of green peas. Pick up a chocolate cake from the bakery or freezer section of your supermarket for dessert.

Quick Tip:

Although I call for cooking the Stroganoff in the slow cooker, it also can be cooked for a much shorter period on the stove. (And, if you're like me, you're not always organized enough in the morning to get the slow cooker going!) Simply combine the cream of mushroom soup, canned beef broth, mushrooms and meatballs and bring to a boil. Reduce the heat and simmer for 20 to 30 minutes. Stir the sour cream mixture into the meatballs 10 minutes before serving.

Skillet Chili Mac

Chili Mac is a Cincinnati tradition in which spaghetti noodles are topped with chili and shredded cheese. My version contains all the traditional elements, while cutting down on the number of pots and pans necessary in preparation – this cooks up in one large nonstick skillet!

1 pound lean ground beef
2 15-ounce cans seasoned diced tomato sauce for chili
1 15.5-ounce can chili beans with sauce
1 10-ounce can mild Rotel tomatoes
1 cup water
2 cups rotini or gemelli pasta
1 cup shredded sharp cheddar cheese

Skillet Chili Mac

Brown ground beef in a large skillet (that has a tight-fitting lid). Drain well and return to skillet. Stir in remaining ingredients. Bring to a boil. Reduce heat to medium, cover and simmer 20 minutes, until pasta is tender. Sprinkle with the cheese and return lid. Serve when the cheese is melted.

Makes 6 servings.

Serve with: A tossed salad or deli coleslaw. Cool down your palette with some Creamsicles or orange sherbet for dessert.

Grandma's Beef Goulash

Grandma's Beef Goulash

My grandmother, Elizabeth Boros Gage, was the daughter of Hungarian immigrants and a well-known cook in her south-Columbus, Ohio, community. The Women's Guild of The Hungarian Reformed Church still prints a small cookbook that includes many of her delicious Hungarian dishes. From Chicken Paprikas to Cabbage Rolls, she was truly a kitchen genius who prepared everything from scratch. Here, her Hungarian Beef Goulash offers a hearty, flavorful twist on traditional beef stew. The dish can be cooked on the stove, or the ingredients can be tossed together in the slow cooker for an all-day simmer. I love Grandma's Goulash just as it is, but half a cup of sour cream can be stirred in at the end of cooking, for a creamy variation.

2 cups chopped onion
2 pounds lean stew beef
1$^1/_2$ teaspoons salt, or to taste
$^1/_4$ teaspoon freshly ground black pepper
2 teaspoons sweet paprika
$^1/_2$ green bell pepper, left uncut
1$^1/_2$ cups peeled and sliced carrots (about 4 carrots)
1 medium kohlrabi, cut into 1-inch cubes
4 medium potatoes, peeled and cut into 1-inch cubes
1 cup water

Spray a large Dutch oven with nonstick cooking spray. Add onions and brown over medium-high heat, 5 minutes. Stir in beef, salt, pepper and paprika. Place $^1/_2$ bell pepper on top of meat mixture. Bring mixture to a boil, reduce heat to low and simmer 1$^1/_2$ hours.

Add remaining vegetables and 1 cup water and bring to a boil. Reduce heat to medium-low and simmer until vegetables are tender, 20 to 30 minutes more.

Makes 6 servings.

Note: To cook the goulash in a slow cooker, place all ingredients in slow cooker and cook on low for 6 to 8 hours.

Serve with: Good bread from the bakery and a salad of sliced cucumber and onions seasoned with salt, pepper, white vinegar and a bit of sugar. For dessert, accompany vanilla ice cream with "Kind of Linzertorte Cookies" by spreading one pecan cookie (Keebler Pecan Sandies are one brand) with raspberry preserves, then topping with another pecan cookie.

Quick Tip:

Kohlrabi is a member of the broccoli family, and is used in many ethnic cuisines. This light green bulbous vegetable was used in many of my grandmother's recipes, including her fabulous chicken soup. While I had no problem finding it in Augusta-area produce sections, you can opt to leave it out of the recipe.

Stout Stew

My recipe for Stout Stew is delicious, while being exceptionally easy to prepare. Although I consider the stout, a classic Irish beer brewed in Dublin, to be a critical element in the stew, if you would rather cook without alcohol, you could substitute $1/2$ cup strong brewed coffee and 1 cup of water for the beer. The Guinness has a coffee-like flavor, and your stew should taste pretty close to the original version.

Stout Stew

$2^1/_2$ pounds lean stew beef
$1/_2$ teaspoon salt
$1/_2$ teaspoon garlic powder
Freshly ground black pepper, to taste
1 large onion, halved and sliced
1 12-ounce bottle Guinness Extra Stout beer

8 ounces fresh button mushrooms
2 cups baby carrots
1 4-inch stem of rosemary, or 1 teaspoon
  dried rosemary leaves
2 bay leaves
$1/_4$ cup cornstarch
$1/_2$ cup water

Makes 6 servings.

Combine all ingredients except the cornstarch and water in a slow cooker and cook on low for 6 to 8 hours. Combine the cornstarch and water in a bowl and stir into the stew. Cover the slow cooker and allow the stew to cook an additional 10 minutes, until thickened slightly.

Serve with: Mashed potatoes and green peas. Slices of heated bakery apple pie topped with a scoop of vanilla ice cream or frozen yogurt would be a nice dessert.

Reuben Casserole

Reuben Casserole

St. Patrick's Day: The one day of the year when corned beef and cabbage and green beer make an appearance. And although St. Patrick's Day is an Irish holiday, the rest of us use it as an excuse to wear green and have a little fun. Keeping with the theme ingredients of corned beef and cabbage, I've adopted Reuben sandwiches as my St. Patrick's Day fare. Here, the Reuben ingredients are layered in a delicious, simple casserole.

12 ounces sliced deli corned beef, chopped
2 cups rye bread cubes
1 16-ounce can sauerkraut, well drained
1 8-ounce bottle regular, reduced-fat or fat-free Thousand Island salad dressing
$1^1/_2$ cup shredded Swiss cheese

Preheat oven to 350 degrees. Layer half of ingredients in a baking dish in order listed. Repeat with remaining ingredients. Bake, uncovered, for 25 minutes.

Makes 4 servings.

Serve with: A fresh fruit salad. Green beer is strictly optional! But, you can add a touch of green to your meal with some instant pistachio pudding for dessert.

Teriyaki Flank Steak

Flank steak is a fairly inexpensive cut, which can be tough if not marinated, then cooked and sliced properly. This Teriyaki Flank Steak recipe offers a quick teriyaki marinade made from pantry staples that's a cut above the bottled version from the supermarket.

$^1/_3$ cup soy sauce
$^1/_3$ cup honey
2 tablespoons cider vinegar
1 teaspoon chopped garlic
  (1 large clove)

1 teaspoon ground ginger
8 drops Tabasco sauce
One $1^1/_2$-pound flank steak

Teriyaki Flank Steak

Combine all ingredients except steak in a gallon-sized zip-top plastic bag. Squeeze well. Add steak and marinate several hours or overnight. Grill or broil 4 to 5 minutes per side, or until internal temperature registers 125-130 degrees on an instant-read meat thermometer. Place steak on a cutting board and let rest 5 minutes before slicing against the grain and serving.

Makes 6 servings.

Serve with: Packaged long grain and wild rice mix, steamed broccoli and sliced tomatoes drizzled with vinaigrette.

Quick Tip:

Besides marinating the steak to give it added flavor, flank steak benefits from being cooked to rare or medium-rare. Otherwise, you'll end up with chewy beef. Another trick to getting maximum tenderness out of this tougher cut of beef is slicing it against the grain. Slicing with a sharp carving knife at a slight angle will help keep your steak as tender as possible.

Flank steak can be grilled or broiled in the oven for about four minutes per side. Indoor, counter-top grills (the famous boxer variety) also can be used. Just cut the cooking time to about 5 minutes total, since these popular kitchen appliances heat from both sides at once. You'll know your steak is done to rare/medium-rare when an instant-read meat thermometer registers between 125 and 130 degrees.

Another Quick Tip:

Your leftover steak and rice make a wonderful salad when marinated artichoke hearts, sliced black olives and chopped green onion are added. I'll often prepare extra steak and rice to make this salad for another meal later in the week!

Carbonara Frittata

Pasta alla Carbonara is one of my favorite dishes. Strands of pasta coated in a bacon and egg sauce with a hefty sprinkling of freshly grated Parmesan is pure comfort food to me. My love of the classic dish, along with some leftover spaghetti noodles in the refrigerator, led me to create another way to enjoy the flavors of the original in a Carbonara Frittata.

Carbonara Frittata

8 ounces spaghetti noodles, cooked and drained
4 slices bacon, diced
1 15-ounce container part-skim ricotta cheese
$^1/_4$ cup dry white wine, optional

1 4-ounce package 6-cheese Italian shredded cheeses*
3 large eggs, beaten
Salt and freshly ground black pepper, to taste

Preheat oven to 350 degrees.

Place the spaghetti in a large bowl and set aside. Sauté the diced bacon in a skillet over medium-high heat until crisp and browned. Set aside to cool.

Combine the ricotta cheese, wine, 1$^1/_2$ cups of the shredded cheese and the eggs in a medium bowl. Stir into the spaghetti. Pour the bacon and drippings over the spaghetti and toss lightly to combine. Season to taste with salt and pepper and toss again. Place the mixture in a 9-inch round ovenproof baking dish and top with the remaining shredded cheese. Bake for 30 minutes. Cut into wedges and serve.

Makes 6 servings.

*1 cup shredded mozzarella cheese and 1 cup shredded Parmesan cheese can be substituted for the 6-cheese Italian shredded cheeses.

Serve with: Salad greens topped with sliced tomatoes and your favorite vinaigrette or cooked frozen green peas. For dessert, top angel food cake slices with instant vanilla pudding and fresh berries. (The frittata also is delicious served as the centerpiece of a special brunch, with a fruit salad on the side.)

Cuban Sandwiches

Cuban Sandwiches

Grinders, hoagies, subs, cheese steaks and po' boys are all versions of the same thing: sliced meat and cheese on a roll. What they're called depends on what part of the country you visit. Now, you can add another name to your list. The Cuban Sandwich has worked its way up from Miami to be present on menus across the country. Make these sandwiches super quick by purchasing thickly sliced ham and roast pork from your supermarket's deli. (If your favorite supermarket doesn't carry roast pork, feel free to substitute in-store roasted turkey breast.) And, look for sliced pickles in a jar rather than slicing them yourself.

$^1/_2$ **pound deli ham, sliced thick**
4 submarine rolls, 6 inches long, split
4 tablespoons Dijon-mayonnaise*
16 thin slices of dill pickle

$^1/_2$ **pound roasted pork, sliced thick**
8 slices Muenster cheese
2 tablespoons butter, softened

Heat a large skillet over medium-high. Add a single layer of sliced ham and fry until browned. Turn over and brown on other side. Repeat with remaining slices, and set aside when all are browned.

Spread the Dijon-mayonnaise on the split rolls. Divide the ham, roast pork, cheese and pickles evenly between the rolls. Spread butter on the outsides of the rolls.

Heat griddle or large skillet over medium-high heat. When hot, add 2 sandwiches. Top with a heavy cast iron skillet or heavy pot, and cook until golden, about 3 minutes. Turn sandwiches,

weigh down and grill until golden, 3 minutes more. Repeat with remaining sandwiches, cut in half and serve.

Makes 4 servings.

*Dijonnaise was used for testing purposes. However, you can prepare your own Dijon-mayonnaise by mixing 2 tablespoons Dijon mustard with 2 tablespoons mayonnaise.

Serve with: Baby carrots or coleslaw and chips. Look for prepared flan (usually found near the refrigerated puddings) at your supermarket for dessert.

Pesto-Beef Hero

The notion of a "sandwich supper" gets taken to new heights with this family-sized Pesto-Beef Hero. And, serving up one huge sandwich instead of individual sandwiches makes a "sandwich supper" more fun!

1 round loaf sourdough bread
$^1/_2$ cup reduced-fat mayonnaise
4 tablespoons prepared pesto
   sauce
1 pound sliced deli roast beef

1 7-ounce jar roasted red bell
   peppers, drained well
4 ounces sliced Provolone cheese
$^1/_2$ bag prepared Hearts
   of Romaine lettuce

Slice loaf of bread in half. Remove some of the soft bread, leaving a 1-inch bread shell.

Combine the mayonnaise and pesto in a small bowl. Spread on both halves of the bread shell.

Layer roast beef, roasted peppers, cheese and Romaine over the bottom bread shell. Top with the top bread shell and serve immediately or wrap securely in heavy-duty aluminum foil or place in a zip-top plastic bag and refrigerate for up to 1 day.

Makes 6 servings.

Serve with: Sides of fresh fruit and potato chips. For dessert, serve some jumbo chocolate chip cookies from the bakery.

Pesto-Beef Hero

Quick Tip:

Use this recipe as a base for other hero sandwiches. A giant ham and Swiss sandwich on a round of country white bread spread with Thousand Island dressing and layered with lettuce and tomatoes would be great. Make a hero with a Mexican twist by combining some prepared salsa with light mayonnaise, spreading on a round of French or Italian bread and layering with deli turkey, jalapeño Jack cheese, shredded lettuce, sliced black olives and tomatoes.

Ham and Cheese Quiche

Quiche is the perfect entrée during any busy season. It's versatile in both preparation and ingredients. And, it can be baked early in the day and refrigerated, then reheated in individual portions in the microwave. A whole quiche also can be reheated in the oven. My children love the simplicity of this combination of diced ham, cheddar cheese and eggs. And it makes a terrific entrée morning, noon and night!

1 9-inch frozen deep-dish pie crust
4 ounces diced smoked ham
2 cups shredded cheddar cheese
4 eggs
1 cup whipping cream, half and half or milk
$^1/_2$ teaspoon salt
$^1/_4$ teaspoon freshly ground black pepper

Preheat oven to 375 degrees. Sprinkle ham and cheese over the bottom of the prepared frozen pie crust. Whisk eggs, whipping cream, half and half or skim milk, salt and pepper in a medium bowl and pour over other ingredients. Place on a baking sheet and bake for 40 to 50 minutes, until center is puffed. Allow to rest 5 minutes before slicing into wedges.

Makes 4 to 6 servings.

Serve with: Fruit kebabs and muffins, or a tossed salad and rolls.

Quick Tip:

Use your creativity to develop your own favorite quiches. The custard proportions should remain the same, but fillings could include bacon and Swiss with sautéed chopped scallions or onions. Browned sausage, ground beef, shrimp or crab meat are other options as well.

Crockpot Carnitas

Crockpot Carnitas

In the United States we generally associate Mexican food with beef tacos in crispy shells, but I've discovered there's a whole world of wonderful authentic Mexican home cooking. Carnitas are a popular Mexican dish, which call for browning a cubed pork roast in a pot, and then adding sliced onion and jalapeños, large strips of orange rind and a can of Dr. Pepper or Coca-Cola. The browned meat simmered for several hours, then was shredded with a fork and served on flour tortillas.

My version has all the traditional elements, with the time-saving help of slow cooker cooking. Instead of a pork roast, I use pork tenderloin to keep the fat grams low, and preparation time short. Wrap the finished shredded pork in flour tortillas, top with some Pico De Gallo and you're on your way to Mexico!

$1^{1}/_{2}$ to 2 pounds pork tenderloin, cut into 2-inch cubes
1 medium onion, peeled and sliced
1 fresh jalapeño pepper, seeded and sliced
3 large strips orange peel, optional

1 12-ounce can Dr. Pepper, Mr. Pibb or Coca-Cola
16 Flour tortillas
Pico de Gallo (see recipe below)

Combine pork, onion, jalapeño, orange peel and soda in a slow cooker. Cover and cook on low for 6 to 8 hours. Uncover and shred the meat using two forks. Serve on the flour tortillas and top with the Pico de Gallo, if desired.

Makes 8 servings.

Pico de Gallo

1 large tomato, cored and chopped
1 medium onion, finely chopped
$^{1}/_{2}$ jalapeño pepper, seeded and finely chopped,
    or to taste

$^{1}/_{2}$ cup fresh cilantro leaves, chopped
1 tablespoon fresh lime juice
Salt and freshly ground black pepper, to taste

Combine all ingredients in a small bowl, seasoning to taste with salt and pepper. Cover and refrigerate until ready to use.

Makes $1^{1}/_{2}$ cups

Serve with: Packaged Mexican rice and a tossed salad dressed with a creamy salsa dressing. Just combine $^{1}/_{2}$ cup each of salsa and sour cream with $^{1}/_{2}$ teaspoon garlic salt and 1 tablespoon red wine vinegar. Caramel ice cream (dulce de leche) would be a fitting dessert.

Minute Mu Shu

Chinese takeout is a quick way to get supper on the table. But, what if I told you that you could whip up a great Chinese meal at home quicker than a trip to the takeout? You can, with my recipe for Minute Mu Shu. Your supermarket has a bevy of convenience products that can help you prepare this classic Chinese takeout dish at home in minutes, and you only need a knife for two ingredients.

Minute Mu Shu

1 teaspoon vegetable oil
2 boneless pork loin chops, trimmed of fat and thinly sliced (about 8 ounces)
1 bunch scallions, washed, dried and diagonally sliced into 1-inch strips
1 16-ounce bag shredded cabbage for coleslaw
1 cup shredded carrots, optional

1 cup sliced fresh mushrooms
1 teaspoon minced garlic (1 large clove)
$^1/_2$ cup teriyaki baste and glaze
$^1/_4$ cup water
8 flour tortillas
Hoisin sauce (see Quick Tip below)

Place a large skillet with a tight-fitting lid over medium-high heat. Add the oil and sliced pork and sauté 1 minute. Add the scallions, cabbage, carrots (if desired) and mushrooms. Stir well, and sauté 3 minutes. While the pork and vegetables cook, combine the garlic, Teriyaki baste and water in a small bowl. Pour over pork and vegetable mixture, stirring well. Reduce heat, cover and simmer for 7 to 10 minutes, until vegetables are very tender. Spread the tortillas with desired amount of Hoisin sauce, and top with some of the pork and cabbage mixture.

Makes 4 servings.

Serve with: Soup made from canned broth that's heated with a few sliced mushrooms and scallions. (You can use the Oriental broth available at some supermarkets, or reduced-sodium chicken or beef broth.) Sliced fresh Asian pears also would be a refreshing addition to this Chinese meal, in place of a traditional fruit salad. Pick up some fortune cookies and vanilla frozen yogurt for dessert.

Quick Tip:

Many of the ingredients in this recipe come ready-to-use. Look for shredded cabbage for coleslaw in bags near the prepared salad greens; minced garlic in jars; and prepared Oriental sauces, such as Hoisin, in the Oriental foods section of your supermarket.

Another Quick Tip:

While Mu Shu Pork is one of my favorite Chinese take-out meals, you can create Mu Shu Chicken or Shrimp just as easily. Substitute two thinly sliced boneless, skinless chicken breast halves or half a pound of medium shrimp for the pork. Follow the recipe exactly if you're substituting chicken, but when substituting shrimp, add it last and cook until it just turns pink.

Dave's Pepperoni Cheese Loaf

It's an everyday cooking quandary. What to prepare for dinner that will please both the children and adults? If that isn't enough to make menu planning difficult, throw in children with different preferences and you may just throw in the towel. Here's a recipe my brother, Dave Gage of Ormond Beach, Fla., learned in his middle-school home economics class that'll please the whole family!

Dave's Pepperoni Cheese Loaf

1 loaf frozen bread dough, thawed
1 egg, beaten
$^1/_2$ cup grated Parmesan cheese
3 ounces sliced pepperoni

2 cups shredded mozzarella cheese
$^1/_2$ teaspoon dried oregano
Spaghetti or marinara sauce

Preheat oven to 375 degrees.

Roll bread dough into a large rectangle on a lightly floured surface. Combine egg and Parmesan cheese in a small bowl and spread over bread dough. Layer pepperoni, then Mozzarella cheese. Sprinkle with oregano. Roll up jellyroll style into a small loaf. Place on a baking sheet and bake for 30 minutes.

While loaf is baking, warm spaghetti or marinara sauce in a saucepan over medium heat. Slice the loaf into wedges and top with some of the sauce.

Makes 6 servings.

Serve with: Carrot and celery sticks with ranch dressing for dipping. Make banana splits for dessert.

Quick Tip:

Using frozen bread dough requires a bit of pre-planning. An overnight stint in the refrigerator and about 15 minutes sitting out at room temperature are all that's required. When life is really crazed and you can't think that far ahead, simply substitute a tube of prepared pizza crust from your supermarket's refrigerator section.

Another Quick Tip:

Although the recipe calls for pepperoni, you can use your favorite pizza toppings instead. Browned sausage meat, chopped ham and even cooked, cubed chicken can be substituted. Vegetable additions might include chopped spinach (simply defrost a 10-ounce package of frozen chopped spinach and drain well), sliced bell peppers or mushrooms.

Pink Prosciutto Penne

This recipe is based on my version of Penne with Vodka Sauce, a classic Italian preparation that I first sampled while on my honeymoon in St. Martin. Since I rarely have vodka on hand, this delicious pasta entrée has become Pink Prosciutto Penne. The vodka in the sauce was replaced with white wine, but chicken broth can be substituted. The prosciutto, along with some diced onion, red pepper flakes and Italian seasoned tomatoes give this dish loads of flavor. It's easy, elegant and perfect for entertaining!

8 ounces dried penne pasta
2 tablespoons olive oil
2 ounces thinly sliced prosciutto, chopped*
1 medium onion, chopped (about 1 cup)
$^1/_4$ teaspoon dried red pepper flakes, or more to taste
$^1/_2$ cup dry white wine**

1 14.5-ounce can diced tomatoes seasoned with
   basil, garlic and oregano, undrained
1 cup fat-free half and half***
2 teaspoons cornstarch
Freshly grated Romano, Parmesan or Asiago cheese
Chopped fresh parsley, for garnish

Bring a large pot of salted water to a boil. Add the pasta and cook according to package directions.

While pasta cooks, prepare the sauce. Heat the olive oil in a large skillet. Add the chopped prosciutto, onion and dried red pepper flakes and sauté until golden, about 5 minutes. Remove the pan from the burner and add the wine. Return the pan to the burner and stir, loosening up any browned bits from the bottom of the pan and reducing by half, about 2 minutes. Add the tomatoes and bring to a boil, reducing juices slightly, about 2 minutes.

In a bowl, dissolve the cornstarch into the fat-free half and half and stir into the sauce. Simmer 5 minutes, until sauce is thickened slightly.
Drain the pasta and return to the pot. Toss with the sauce and pour out onto a large platter. Sprinkle with the grated cheese and chopped parsley.

Makes 4 servings.

Serve with: Mixed greens, diced tomatoes and cucumbers tossed with your favorite Italian vinaigrette. Look for prepared Tiramisu in your supermarket's bakery for an Italian dessert.

*Prosciutto, Italian-style cured bacon, can be found at most supermarket deli counters.

**Chicken broth may be substituted for the white wine.

***Land O' Lakes fat-free half and half is available at most grocery stores in the diary case alongside the whipping cream, half and half and nondairy creamers. Whipping cream or half and half may be substituted. Just omit the cornstarch from the recipe.

Pink Prosciutto Penne

Pizza Pasta Casserole

Pizza Pasta Casserole

Most children I know are picky eaters. But there's one thing they all seem to like: Pizza. My Pizza Pasta Casserole combines the flavors of their favorite pepperoni pizza without a visit from the delivery man! And, using turkey pepperoni and part-skim mozzarella makes it a heart healthy entrée.

8 ounces dried spaghetti, cooked according
   to package directions
1 6-ounce package regular or turkey pepperoni, divided
2 teaspoons olive oil
1 teaspoon crushed fresh garlic (1 large clove)
1 26.5-ounce jar prepared spaghetti sauce
2 cups shredded part-skim mozzarella cheese

Preheat oven to 350 degrees. Spray a large baking dish with nonstick spray and set aside.

Set aside 15 slices of the pepperoni, and chop the remaining pepperoni coarsely. Heat the olive oil in a large skillet over medium heat. Add the garlic and pepperoni and sauté until pepperoni begins to brown, about 3 minutes. Stir in spaghetti sauce and bring to a boil. Reduce heat and simmer 10 minutes.

Stir cooked spaghetti into the sauce and pour all into the prepared baking dish. Sprinkle with the shredded cheese and place the remaining pepperoni over the top. Bake for 30 minutes, until heated through and cheese is melted.

Makes 6 servings.

Serve with: Cooked carrots and garlic bread. Whip up some instant chocolate pudding for dessert.

Barb's Cheeseburger Pie

If you read a school lunch menu you begin to think the four food groups for children must be pizza, chicken nuggets, corn dogs and cheeseburgers. Since my children usually like to purchase lunch at school when these items are on the menu, they rarely appear on the table at home. However, I'm always looking for meals that will please both husband and children. Here, I've taken the lead from my next-door neighbor, Barbara Mysona. With three boys and a hard-working husband, Barbara pleases both the picky appetites of her sons and hungry husband. Her simple Cheeseburger Pie fits the bill, providing a warm, hearty dish with a taste combination that the kids love.

1 package reduced-fat
   crescent roll dough
1 pound lean ground beef
$1/2$ teaspoon salt
$1/2$ teaspoon chili powder
$1/4$ teaspoon freshly ground
   black pepper
$1/2$ cup dry breadcrumbs
1 16-ounce can tomato
   sauce
$1/4$ cup chopped onion,
   optional,
   or $1/2$ teaspoon onion
   powder

1 egg
$1/4$ cup milk
$1/2$ teaspoon salt
$1/2$ teaspoon dry mustard
$1/2$ teaspoon Worcestershire
   sauce
2 cups shredded cheddar
   cheese

Preheat oven to 425 degrees.

Line pie plate with the crescent roll dough, pressing to seal. Crimp edges.

Brown the ground beef in a large skillet and drain well. Stir in salt, chili powder, pepper, dry breadcrumbs, tomato sauce and onion or onion powder. Spread over dough in pie plate.

Combine egg, milk, salt, dry mustard, Worcestershire and cheese in a medium bowl. Spread over meat mixture.

Bake pie for 30 minutes, until crust is golden brown and cheese mixture is bubbly.

Makes 6 servings.

Mediterranean Strata

Put this delicious egg, sausage and bread casserole together before heading off to bed and you'll awaken to something delicious in the morning. Just pop this Mediterranean version of everyone's favorite sausage breakfast casserole in the oven, and serve with a big fruit salad for breakfast or brunch, or with a Caesar salad for lunch or dinner.

$1/2$ cup sundried tomatoes, not oil packed
12 ounces Italian sausage, casings removed
$3^1/2$ cups 1 percent milk
8 large eggs
1 tablespoon fresh or 1 teaspoon dried thyme
$1^1/2$ teaspoons onion salt

$1/4$ teaspoon freshly ground black pepper
10 ounces French bread, cut into 1-inch cubes
$1/2$ cup grated Parmesan cheese
1 cup grated part-skim mozzarella cheese
2 ounces crumbled goat or feta cheese, optional

In a microwave-safe bowl, reconstitute the tomatoes in the microwave, covered in water, for 3 minutes. Set aside to soften, then drain well and chop.

Heat a large skillet over medium-high heat. Crumble the sausage into the skillet and cook, stirring, until done. Drain well.

Spray a 9-by-13-inch glass baking dish with non-stick cooking spray.

Combine the milk, eggs, thyme, onion salt and pepper in a large bowl. Add tomatoes, sausage, bread cubes and Parmesan cheese. Pour into prepared baking dish. Cover and refrigerate for 4 hours or overnight.

Heat oven to 375 degrees.

Bake the strata, uncovered, for 45 minutes. Remove from oven and sprinkle with the mozzarella and goat or feta cheese, if desired, and bake an additional 5 minutes, until cheeses are melted. Cool on a rack 5 minutes before cutting and serving.

Makes 10 servings

6

Pepper-Crusted Tuna Steaks with Gorgonzola Cream Sauce

fish & seafood

Pepper-Crusted Tuna Steaks with Gorgonzola Cream Sauce

Beautiful sashimi-grade tuna steaks behind the seafood counter at my supermarket prompted me to come up with this special recipe. Rather than turn to my usual Oriental marinade for tuna steaks, I chose to play up the tuna's steak-like quality and turned to a classic steak preparation, Steak Au Poivre (steak coated in cracked peppercorns). Then, I discovered that most supermarkets now carry already crumbled Gorgonzola cheese in the dairy case. I snatched up a package, along with a half pint of half and half, and my meal was planned. Serve this as a romantic dinner for two!

2 6-ounce fresh tuna steaks
1 tablespoon coarsely ground or cracked black pepper
1 tablespoon butter

1 tablespoon brandy or cognac
1 cup half and half
4 ounces crumbled Gorgonzola cheese

Place the ground pepper in a plate and dip the top and bottom of each tuna steak in the black pepper, coating well. Heat a large heavy skillet over medium-high heat. Add the tuna steaks and sear 5 minutes per side. Remove the steaks to a plate and place in a warm (200 to 250 degrees) oven.

Add the butter to the skillet, and whisk well, loosening any browned bits remaining in the pan. Remove from the heat and add the brandy or cognac. Boil over high heat until liquid is almost evaporated. Add the half and half and bring to a boil, reduce heat and simmer until reduced by half, about 5 minutes. Stir in the Gorgonzola and remove from the heat. Top each steak with some of the sauce, and serve.

Makes 2 servings.

Serve with: Blanched new potatoes and green beans tossed in a skillet with butter, salt, pepper and thyme. Plate the dish restaurant-style, by placing some of the new potatoes and green beans on the plate, topping with a seared tuna steak, and drizzling with the Gorgonzola sauce. Whip up some instant chocolate mousse as a decadent ending to a decadent meal.

Quick Tip:

New potatoes and green beans are wonderful accompaniments to many entrees, and they can be prepared almost completely ahead. Cook the new potatoes and green beans in separate pots of salted water until just tender, drain them and set aside until just before dinner. Then, right before serving, give the vegetables a brief sauté in a hot skillet with butter, salt and pepper and thyme.

Bond's Low Country Boil

Cooking in a huge pot over a gas burner out in the front yard for all the neighbors to see is a "guy thing." At least it is at my house, where my husband, Bond, is the king of big-pot cooking. Low Country Boil is one of his favorite big-pot meals. So, when he's ready to do a boil, I relinquish my role as head chef, spread some newspapers on the kitchen table and get ready to dig in.

Water
$^3/_4$ cup salt
1 16-ounce bag dry crab boil
1 tablespoon liquid shrimp and crab boil
2 heads garlic, unpeeled and cut in half horizontally
2 lemons cut in half

1 yellow onion, peeled and quartered
10 small red potatoes, washed and halved
1 pound andouille or Polish sausage,
   cut into 2-inch pieces
4 ears of corn, cleaned and cut in half
1$^1/_2$ pounds large shrimp, unpeeled

Fill a 6 to 8-quart stock pot $^3/_4$ full with water. Add the salt, dry and liquid crab boils, garlic, lemons and onion. Cover and bring to a boil.

Remove the lid and add the potatoes and cook for 5 minutes. Add the sausage and corn, cover and bring to a boil and cook for 5 minutes more. Add the shrimp and turn the flame off. Let sit 15 minutes. Drain and serve.

Makes 6 servings.

Serve with: Garlic bread, melted butter and cocktail sauce complete Bond's seafood feast. Whip up some Strawberry Ice Cream Shortcakes for dessert. Toss fresh sliced strawberries with a bit of sugar, then refrigerate. Top store-bought shortcake rounds with scoops of vanilla ice cream, then top with the sliced strawberries.

Skillet Shrimp Creole

Each February there's a huge Mardi Gras celebration in New Orleans. The pre-Lent celebration, which began in 1699, gives me a great excuse to cook up some Creole and Cajun cuisine. This recipe is a cinch to prepare, and delivers just the right Creole flavor – not too spicy!

$^1/_2$ pound turkey or pork kielbasa, diced
1 bag seasoning blend
1 28-ounce can diced tomatoes, undrained
1 12-ounce bottle chili sauce

2 tablespoons Worcestershire sauce
$^1/_2$ teaspoon salt
1 teaspoon Cajun seasoning
1 pound medium shrimp, peeled and deveined

Skillet Shrimp Creole

Sauté the kielbasa in a large nonstick skillet until browned. Remove from skillet and set aside. Add the seasoning blend to the skillet and sauté until vegetables are tender, about 5 minutes. Stir in tomatoes, chili sauce, Worcestershire sauce, salt and Cajun seasoning and bring to a boil. Return the kielbasa to the skillet, reduce heat and simmer, covered, for 20 minutes. Add the shrimp and cook until the shrimp are just pink.

Makes 6 servings.

Serve with: Hot cooked white rice, crusty bread and a green salad tossed with your favorite vinaigrette. During Mardi Gras season, finish your meal with a King Cake from your favorite bakery. Otherwise, serve with store-prepared brownies sprinkled with powdered sugar.

Apple Bread

—By Suzanne Beane, Waterville, Maine

TERESA BLACKBURN

1 cup sugar

2 eggs

4 1/2 teaspoons evaporated milk

1/2 cup vegetable oil

2 cups all-purpose flour

1 teaspoon baking soda

1/2 teaspoon salt

1 cup chopped unpeeled apple

Sugar and cinnamon (optional)

Serves 12

1. Preheat oven to 350F. Grease a 9 x 5-inch loaf pan.

2. Combine sugar, eggs, milk and oil; beat until well combined. Add flour, soda and salt; mix well. Stir in chopped apple. Pour into prepared pan. Sprinkle sugar and cinnamon on top, if desired. Bake about 1 hour.

Shrimp Pad Thai

Pad Thai is perhaps the most popular Thai dish in the United States., and I developed this quick and easy version as a toast to 2000 Masters Champion Vijay Singh, who requested a Thai meal for his Champions Dinner. While the pursuit of Thai ingredients used to require a trip to an Oriental market, today many Thai staples can be found on the shelves of your local supermarket.

Shrimp Pad Thai

8 ounces dry linguine
$1/4$ cup Thai fish sauce
$1/4$ cup granulated sugar
$1/4$ cup white vinegar
1 teaspoon paprika
$1/2$ teaspoon red pepper flakes

Cook linguine according to package directions, drain and set aside.

Combine fish sauce, granulated sugar, vinegar, paprika and red pepper flakes in a small bowl. Stir to dissolve the sugar. Set aside.

Heat the vegetable oil in a large skillet over medium-high heat. Add the green onions, garlic and shrimp and sauté until shrimp turn pink, 2 to 4 minutes. Add eggs and cook, stirring constantly, for 1 minute or until cooked. Add the linguine and fish sauce mixture and cook, stirring constantly, for 2 to 3 minutes. Transfer to a serving platter and sprinkle with chopped peanuts.

2 tablespoons vegetable oil
3 green onions, sliced into 1-inch pieces
1 teaspoon chopped garlic (1 large clove)
$1/2$ pound medium shrimp, peeled and deveined
2 eggs, beaten
Roasted peanuts, finely chopped, for garnish

Makes 4 servings.

Serve with: A salad of sliced cucumbers tossed with seasoned rice vinegar (which can be found with the other vinegars in most supermarkets) is the perfect accompaniment. Ripe mangos, either on their own or with vanilla ice cream, would make a nice dessert.

Quick Tip:

Pad Thai is the perfect example of true Thai flavors. It is subtly sweet, tart and salty all at once. Traditional Pad Thai recipes call for cooked chicken or roast pork in place of or along with the shrimp, so feel free to improvise. Fresh bean sprouts also are often tossed in with the noodles before serving.

Lemon Shrimp Risotto

Lemon Shrimp Risotto

Mention Italian food, and pasta usually comes to mind. But in some parts of Italy, rice, particularly Arborio rice, is the "starch supreme." I'm not talking about plain, boiled rice, however. I'm talking about risotto, a creamy Italian rice dish that became popular on the American culinary scene about 10 years ago. I've taken shortcuts here so that you're not standing over your risotto stirring your arm off like an Italian grandma, but the resulting dish comes close to the labor-intensive classic.

2 tablespoons butter
$^1/_2$ cup chopped onion
1 teaspoon minced garlic (1 large clove)
2 cups Arborio rice
2 14.5-ounce cans reduced-sodium chicken broth

1 lemon, zested and juiced (about 1 teaspoon lemon zest and 2 tablespoons lemon juice)
3 green onions, chopped, divided
Salt and freshly ground black pepper, to taste
1 pound medium shrimp, peeled and deveined

Melt butter in a large saucepan over medium heat. Add onion and sauté until tender, about 3 minutes. Add garlic and rice and sauté 2 minutes. Add chicken broth, lemon juice and half of the chopped green onions. Bring to a boil, then reduce heat and simmer, covered, for 15 minutes.

Combine shrimp and remaining green onions in a medium bowl. Season to taste with salt and ground black pepper. Stir shrimp and green onions into rice. Cover and simmer on low for 3 to 5 minutes, until shrimp are cooked.

Makes 6 servings.

Serve with: Sautéed fresh spinach. For dessert, scoop Rocky Road ice cream into sugar cones for a chocolaty childhood treat.

Quick Tip:

Sautéed spinach is a snap with washed and ready bags of fresh spinach. Look for 10-ounce bags in the produce section. Then, sauté a teaspoon of minced garlic in a bit of olive oil in a large skillet or Dutch oven. Add the whole bag of spinach, season with salt and black pepper, and cover with a tight-fitting lid. Stir the spinach every two minutes or so, until it's completely wilted.

Hushpuppy Catfish

Our fun friends John and Susan Crocker, and their three children, moved from Augusta to Tennessee, and although we miss them terribly, we're blessed to have lots of great memories, and a stash of Susan's excellent recipes. Susan came up with the idea of using hushpuppy mix as a breading for pan-fried fish, and I've used her idea to develop this easy, low fat oven-baked recipe.

Hushpuppy Catfish

4 6-ounce catfish fillets
Salt and freshly ground black pepper, to taste
Butter flavored cooking spray
³/₄ cup prepared hushpuppy mix
Lemon wedges, for accompaniment

Preheat oven to 500 degrees.

Spread hushpuppy mix on a plate, and spray a baking pan with the cooking spray. Set aside.

Season fish fillets with salt and pepper on both sides. Then, spray both sides of fillets with butter flavored cooking spray. Dip fillets into hushpuppy mix, pressing fish into mix and coating well. Place fillets in prepared pan and mist with additional cooking spray.

When oven is hot, place pan in upper third of oven and bake for 5 to 10 minutes, depending on thickness of the fillets. Serve with lemon wedges.

Makes 4 servings.

Serve with: When pairing side dishes with your Hushpuppy Fish, think "fish fry". Cheese grits (quick grits topped with grated cheese) and coleslaw are the logical choices. Add some sautéed cherry or grape tomatoes for a splash of color on the plate. Key Lime Pie from your supermarket would be a fitting dessert.

Quick Tip:

Catfish isn't your only option with this recipe, as other thin, white fillets also work well. Sole, tilapia, flounder or trout all pair beautifully with the hushpuppy coating. Simply pick the freshest white-fleshed fish available at your grocery store or seafood market.

Another Quick Tip:

The essential ingredient in perfect baked fish is a hot oven and a kitchen timer. A basic rule-of-thumb for baking is 10 minutes per inch of thickness. Catfish fillets, in general will take about 8 minutes to bake, while thin fillets like sole or tilapia will bake up in about 5 minutes.

Lemony Shrimp Picatta

Lemony Shrimp Picatta

Why wait in a long restaurant line when you can whip up this restaurant-worthy shrimp entrée practically in minutes? The recipe's perfect for celebrating a family member or friend's birthday, or serve it to Mom on Mother's Day!

1 cup dry orzo pasta, cooked according
   to package directions
2 tablespoons olive oil, divided
Salt and freshly ground black pepper
2 teaspoons minced garlic (2-3 large cloves)
$1^1/_2$ pounds medium shrimp, peeled and deveined

$^1/_2$ red bell pepper, diced
$^1/_4$ cup chopped fresh parsley
2 lemons, zested and juiced
1 cup white wine or chicken broth
4 tablespoons butter, cut into 4 pieces
$^1/_3$ cup capers, drained

Drizzle 1 tablespoon of the olive oil over the orzo and season to taste with salt and pepper. Place on a serving platter and set aside.

Heat the remaining 1 tablespoon of olive oil and garlic in a large skillet over medium-high heat. Add the shrimp and sauté 1 minute, until slightly caramelized on one side. Turn the shrimp over and add the diced bell pepper and chopped parsley. Season to taste with salt and pepper and sauté until shrimp are done, about 3 minutes. Spoon shrimp mixture over the orzo and set aside.

Return the skillet to the heat and add the lemon juice and white wine. Bring to a boil and reduce by $^1/_3$. Turn off heat and whisk in the butter, one tablespoon at a time, whisking to incorporate after each addition. When all butter is incorporated, add the lemon rind and capers and pour over the shrimp.

Makes 6 servings.

Serve with: Steamed broccoli or asparagus spears. For dessert, pick up a small chocolate layer cake in the supermarket's freezer section. Garnish each slice with a fresh strawberry or a sprig of fresh mint.

Quick Tip

While I usually cook orzo in chicken broth with liquid-to-orzo ratios similar to the recipe for cooking rice (two parts liquid to one part orzo or rice), for this recipe I'd recommend boiling it in a lot of liquid, then draining and rinsing it under hot water. This removes some of the starch from the orzo so that it won't form a mass of pasta while you prepare your shrimp.

Shrimp and Veggie Alfredo

Shrimp and Veggie Alfredo

This recipe packs great restaurant flavor in a simple-to-prepare shrimp and pasta dish that epitomizes my philosophy that while "quick cooking" is a necessity in our busy times, being "quick" isn't enough. The food has got to taste great. And, this dish does!

1 12-ounce bag stir-fry ready broccoli, carrots
   and snow peas*
1 tablespoon butter or margarine
8 ounces sliced fresh mushrooms
1 red or yellow bell pepper, cored and sliced
1 pound medium shrimp, peeled and deveined
1 teaspoon Cajun seasoning

8 ounces grape or cherry tomatoes
1 16-ounce jar roasted garlic parmesan
   or other Alfredo-style sauce
9 ounces refrigerated "fresh" fettuccine
Freshly ground black pepper, to taste
Freshly grated Parmesan cheese, to taste

Bring a large pot of water to a boil. Place broccoli, carrots and snow peas** in a microwave-safe bowl or container and microwave 3 minutes, until crisp-tender. Drain and set aside.

In a large sauté pan, melt the butter over medium-high heat. Add the mushrooms and bell pepper strips and sauté until mushrooms are golden brown. Season the shrimp with the Cajun seasoning and add to the mushrooms. Sauté 3 minutes.   Add the broccoli, carrots and snow peas, the grape tomatoes and the sauce. Simmer 5 minutes.

Cook the pasta in the water according to package directions. Drain and place on a large platter. Pour the sauce over top, season to taste with the black pepper and sprinkle with the Parmesan cheese.

Makes 6 servings.

*Look for bags of fresh, stir-fry ready vegetables in your supermarket's produce section.

**The vegetables also can be cooked in the boiling water along with the pasta. Drain the pasta and vegetables, and then toss with the sauce.

Serve with: Sliced cucumbers with your favorite vinaigrette would be a great start to your meal, then add some rolls or crusty bread, if you're really hungry, and some refreshing sorbet or Italian ice for dessert.

Red-Eye Shrimp and Grits

Red-Eye Shrimp and Grits

Shrimp and Grits is a classic Charleston dish, with nearly every Charleston restaurant and resident serving up their own unique take on the combination. Variations for the shrimp sauté can be as simple as shrimp, butter and garlic, or elaborate preparations with homemade shrimp stock reductions and whipping cream. My version replicates one I sampled in several Charleston-area restaurants, and includes another Southern tradition, red-eye gravy.

4 ounces country ham or other smoked ham, chopped
1 tablespoon olive oil
8 ounces sliced fresh mushrooms
$1/_2$ teaspoon seasoning salt
$1/_2$ teaspoon dried minced thyme
$1/_2$ cup chopped green onions
2 teaspoons minced garlic (2 large cloves)

1 cup strong coffee
$1/_4$ cup sherry
1 tablespoon cornstarch
1 teaspoon hot pepper sauce, or to taste
1 pound medium shrimp, peeled and deveined
Cooked grits or cheese grits

Sauté country ham in olive oil in a large saucepan over medium-high heat until golden. Add mushrooms, seasoning salt and thyme and sauté until mushrooms are golden, about 3 to 5 minutes. Add green onions and garlic and sauté 3 minutes more.

Combine coffee, sherry, cornstarch and hot sauce in a small bowl. Add to the sauté pan and bring to a boil. Add the shrimp and simmer until cooked, about 2 minutes.

Spoon grits onto individual dinner plates, then divide the Red-Eye Shrimp over the grits.

Makes 4 servings.

Serve with: You can serve the shrimp over plain cooked grits, but it's even better over cheese grits. Toss a salad of mixed greens, diced tomato and avocado with creamy ranch dressing and add a side of crusty French bread. Create individual turtle pies for dessert by scooping coffee ice cream into individual graham cracker crusts and drizzling with hot fudge sauce.

Quick Tip:

My Mother-in-Law, Carol Calloway, taught me how to make delicious Cheese Grits. She cooks up a batch of grits (four to six servings worth), seasons to taste with salt and pepper, and then spreads half of the grits in a greased baking dish. She sprinkles the grits with some shredded sharp cheddar cheese, then tops with the remaining grits, sprinkles with more cheese, places a few dabs of butter (about 2 tablespoons worth) randomly over the top and covers with foil. This can be made ahead, and heated just before serving. Bake at 350 degrees for 20 to 30 minutes, until bubbly. Stir to distribute the cheese just before serving.

My Linguine with White Clam Sauce

I tried many recipes for the popular Italian pasta dish, Linguine with Clam Sauce, but most fell flat in the flavor department. So, I came up with my own version, which until now has been a guarded recipe. It's such a family favorite that my sister, Leslie Marcus, advised me against sharing it, but since that's what I do for a living, here it is! This is a lengthier recipe than most in this book, but once you get the chopping done, the sauce practically cooks itself.

1 pound Linguine pasta, cooked according
   to package directions
$^1/_4$ cup olive oil
$^1/_4$ cup butter
$^1/_2$ cup green onions, minced
$^1/_2$ cup peeled and finely chopped shallots
3 teaspoons minced garlic (5 to 6 cloves)
1 teaspoon dried oregano

Freshly ground black pepper, to taste
$^1/_4$ cup chopped fresh parsley
$1^1/_2$ cups dry white wine
1 14.5-ounce can reduced-sodium chicken broth
4 6.5-ounce cans minced clams,
   drained and juices reserved
Salt to taste
Freshly grated Parmesan cheese, for garnish

Heat a very large skillet over medium-high heat. When hot, add the olive oil and butter. When butter is melted and bubbling, stir in the minced green onions and shallots. Sauté until softened and fragrant, about 5 minutes.

Add the garlic, and sauté until softened, about 2 minutes. Stir in the oregano, black pepper and chopped parsley. Add white wine, chicken stock and reserved juice from the clams and bring to a boil. Reduce heat to medium and simmer, uncovered, until sauce is reduced by $^1/_3$, about 8 to 10 minutes. When sauce is reduced, stir in the minced clams and salt to taste and heat through, being careful not to boil. Serve immediately over the pasta.

Top each serving with the freshly grated Parmesan cheese.

Makes 4 to 6 servings.

Note: The sauce can be made ahead. Prepare to just before adding the clams, cover and refrigerate. Refrigerate the drained clams in a separate airtight container until ready to use. Heat sauce to a simmer, then stir in clams. Let the clams simmer for 2 minutes, and serve immediately.

Serve with: A tossed salad with tomato wedges and cucumber slices with your favorite Italian vinaigrette and slices of crusty bread. For dessert, some Italian ice from the frozen desserts section would be nice.

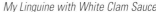

Quick Tip:

One of my favorite gadgets is a hand-held food chopper. You place the ingredients to be chopped on a cutting board, fit the chopper over the items to be chopped and give the chopper a couple of hard presses down. The choppers can be found at most specialty cooking stores, or at linen and kitchenware stores for $20 to $30.

My Linguine with White Clam Sauce

Baked Fish with Roasted Corn and Tomato Remoulade

Baked Fish with Roasted Corn and Tomato Remoulade

I love the ease of oven roasting fish fillets, and developed this recipe when my favorite supermarket seafood department had beautiful pink steelhead trout fillets. The simply prepared fillets are topped with a roasted corn and tomato remoulade sauce, making this truly company worthy. This sauce is wonderful with all types of fish, and is great with fried fish, crab cakes and pan-seared scallops. You'll have leftover sauce, so toss it with some boiled peeled shrimp and serve on a bed of lettuce for a delicious summer salad.

For the Remoulade:
1³/₄ cups corn niblets (2 to 3 ears fresh corn, 1³/₄ cups frozen or 1 11-ounce can drained corn niblets)
1 medium tomato, diced
Salt and freshly ground black pepper
1 tablespoon fresh lemon juice
¹/₄ cup regular or reduced-fat mayonnaise
¹/₄ cup regular or reduced-fat sour cream
2 tablespoons ketchup, chili sauce or cocktail sauce

1 tablespoon grainy or Dijon mustard
2 green onions, chopped
1 teaspoon dry or 1 tablespoon fresh chopped parsley
1 teaspoon Worcestershire sauce

For the fish fillets:*
4 6-ounce steelhead trout fillets
Cajun seasoning, to taste

To prepare the sauce:
Preheat oven to 400 degrees. Spread corn and diced tomatoes on a baking sheet that has been covered with aluminum foil. Season with salt and pepper and roast for 10 to 15 minutes. Remove from oven, scrape into a medium bowl and set aside to cool.

When cool, add the lemon juice, mayonnaise, sour cream, ketchup, mustard, green onions, parsley and Worcestershire. Cover and refrigerate until ready to use.

To prepare the fish:
Preheat oven to 400 degrees. Line a baking sheet with aluminum foil. Place the fish fillets on the baking sheet, skin side down, and sprinkle to taste with the Cajun seasoning. Bake 10 minutes. Remove from baking sheet, slipping a metal spatula between the skin and flesh of the fish, leaving the skin behind.
Place on individual dinner plates and top with ¹/₄ cup of the remoulade sauce.

Makes 4 servings.

Note: Leftover sauce can be refrigerated in a sealed container for up to 1 week.

*Salmon, grouper, mahi mahi or other firm-fleshed fish can be used in place of the Steelhead Trout specified.

Serve with: Toss mixed greens with canned sliced hearts of palm, diced tomatoes, black olives and your favorite tangy vinaigrette and add a side of cooked white rice. For dessert, slice up some French silk pie from your supermarket's refrigerated bakery section.

USS Louisiana's Crawfish Etouffée

It's true that the Navy has the best food — and I should know, having toured both a Naval aircraft carrier and a nuclear submarine. The U.S.S. Louisiana serves up a delicious Shrimp Etouffée. While their recipe serves 100, I've pared the quantity, and the fat, down quite a bit. The recipe now serves 6, and I've replaced the butter or oil-laden traditional roux with an easy "oven roux."

$^1/_2$ cup all-purpose flour
$^1/_2$ green bell pepper
$^1/_2$ yellow bell pepper
$^1/_2$ red bell pepper
1 medium onion
2 teaspoons Old Bay seasoning

1 tablespoon Cajun seasoning
Salt to taste
1 14.5-ounce can reduced-sodium chicken broth
1 pound crawfish tail meat*
1 tablespoon butter or margarine

Preheat oven to 400 degrees.

Sprinkle flour over a baking sheet and bake until lightly browned, for 20 to 25 minutes, stirring every 5 minutes.

While the "oven roux" is browning, dice the bell pepper halves and the onion. Heat a large non-stick skillet that has been coated with nonstick cooking spray over medium-high heat.

Add the vegetables and sauté until wilted and lightly browned, approximately 5 to 8 minutes. Whisk in the browned flour, seasonings and chicken broth and bring to a boil. (Whisk until there are no lumps in the sauce.) Reduce heat and simmer 10 minutes. Stir in the crawfish tail meat and butter and simmer until the crawfish is heated through, about 5 minutes.

Makes 6 servings.

*One pound of medium peeled and deveined shrimp can be substituted for the crawfish tail meat.

Serve with: Hot white rice and a side of steamed broccoli. Crusty French bread would be nice for dipping into the delicious sauce, but isn't essential. For dessert, whip up some instant vanilla pudding and layer with vanilla wafers and sliced bananas for quick banana pudding.

USS Louisiana's Shrimp Etouffée

USS JFK's Shrimp Scampi

USS JFK's Shrimp Scampi

Our friend Capt. Skip Wheeler, who served as the Chief of Staff for the USS John F. Kennedy Battle Group before his retirement from the Navy, invited us aboard this city on the sea. While we toured the ship, Petty Officer 2nd Class Wayne Napples shared this recipe for one of the ship's favorite entrées. The original recipe made 500 servings, but he pared it down to a family-sized four servings for me.

4 tablespoons butter or margarine
2 teaspoons minced garlic (2 large cloves)
$^1/_2$ cup chopped fresh parsley
2 tomatoes, peeled and diced

1 teaspoon fresh lemon juice
Salt and freshly ground black pepper, to taste
1 pound medium shrimp, peeled and deveined
$^1/_2$ cup dry breadcrumbs

Preheat oven to 350 degrees.

Melt butter in a large skillet over medium-high heat. Add garlic and parsley and sauté 3 minutes. Add the chopped tomatoes and lemon juice. Remove from heat and season to taste with salt and pepper.

Season shrimp with salt and pepper and place in the bottom of a 9-inch glass baking dish. Pour tomato mixture over the top. Sprinkle with the breadcrumbs and bake for 15 minutes.

Makes 4 servings.

Serve with: Hot cooked rice and steamed green beans. Drizzle Butter Pecan ice cream with warm caramel sauce for dessert.

Summer Shrimp Pasta

This recipe ran in July of 1999, as a way to use leftover boiled shrimp. Somehow, it was omitted from my first cookbook. I'm including it here for the reader I met at the book's debut who was standing in line for me to sign the book when she realized the recipe wasn't included. My apologies to this loyal reader, and here's the recipe!

Summer Shrimp Pasta was a recipe I created when my fridge presented me with leftover boiled shrimp and a can of chilled artichoke hearts. It's a wonderful, light summer entrée which is good warm, at room temperature or cold as a pasta salad.

9 ounces fresh angel hair or linguine pasta
1 pound cooked and peeled shrimp
1 14.5-ounce can peeled and diced tomatoes, undrained
1 14-ounce can quartered artichoke hearts, drained
1 3.5-ounce can capers, drained
1 tablespoon red wine or balsamic vinegar

$^1/_4$ cup olive oil
$^1/_2$ teaspoon salt
Freshly ground black pepper, to taste
1 4-ounce block Parmesan or Romano cheese, coarsely grated or 1 cup crumbled feta cheese

Bring a large pot of water to a boil over high heat. Add pasta and cook according to package directions. Meanwhile, in a medium bowl, combine the shrimp, undrained tomatoes, artichoke hearts, capers, vinegar, olive oil and seasonings.

Drain the pasta in a colander and return to the pot. Pour sauce over pasta and toss. Add the cheese and toss again. Serve immediately or refrigerate and serve as a cold pasta salad.

Makes 6 servings.

Summer Shrimp Pasta

7

French Toast Casserole

meatless entrées
& side dishes

French Toast Casserole

While my Mother worked as a teacher's aide at Sabal Point Elementary School in Longwood, Fla., I reaped the reward of many delicious recipes. Sue McCullough, an outstanding kindergarten teacher, shared this recipe often with the faculty of the school. It's absolutely amazing how the addition of maple syrup to the custard of eggs, milk, half and half and cream cheese makes the final casserole taste just like French toast!

16 slices dense white sandwich bread,
   cut into $^1/_2$-inch cubes
8 ounces reduced-fat cream cheese, softened
8 large eggs
1$^1/_2$ cups skim milk

$^2/_3$ cups half and half
$^1/_2$ cup maple syrup
$^1/_2$ teaspoon vanilla extract
Powdered sugar, for garnish
Maple syrup, for garnish

Place the bread cubes in a 9-by-13 inch glass baking dish that has been coated with nonstick cooking spray.

Place the cream cheese in a large bowl and beat with an electric mixer until smooth. Add eggs, one at a time, beating well after each addition. Add milk, half-and-half, maple syrup and vanilla and beat until smooth. Pour over top of bread cubes, cover and refrigerate overnight.

Preheat oven to 350 degrees. Remove casserole from refrigerator and let sit at room temperature for 30 minutes. Bake for 50 minutes, until puffed and golden. Slice into individual servings, and top each serving with a sprinkling of powdered sugar and a drizzle of maple syrup, if desired.

Makes 12 servings.

Serve with: Sausage patties and a fresh fruit salad or the scalloped apples below.

Scalloped Apples

Apples are abundant during the fall, so I take advantage of their seasonal bounty in cakes, pies and crisps. While I enjoy these autumn desserts, apples also make an appearance at big weekend breakfasts as Scalloped Apples. These apples are wonderful served alongside waffles, pancakes or French toast with sausage patties or links. Or, serve as a dinner side dish with roast pork or ham.

4 Granny Smith apples, washed, cored and sliced into wedges
1 teaspoon lemon juice
4 tablespoons butter
$^1/_3$ cup brown sugar
$^1/_2$ teaspoon cinnamon
1 pinch freshly grated nutmeg

Toss apple wedges with lemon juice in a bowl and set aside. Heat a large skillet over medium-high and add the butter. When the butter is melted, add the apples and brown sugar. Sauté the apples until they are tender, about 5 minutes. Stir in the cinnamon and nutmeg and serve.

Makes 4 servings.

Baked Eggs in Bread Cups

Baked Eggs in Bread Cups

Cooking breakfast for a crowd can be tricky, but my recipe for Baked Eggs in Bread Cups can almost effortlessly feed a crowd. Slices of your favorite bread (I like soft potato bread) are cut into large rounds, and then are pressed into greased muffin tins. Pressing with the bottom of a glass a bit smaller than the muffin cup will help ease the bread into its place. Chopped green onion and bacon pieces add loads of flavor. And, a topping of packaged béarnaise sauce makes these extra special!

6 slices white bread
6 slices bacon, cooked and crumbled
1 green onion, chopped
$^1/_4$ teaspoon garlic powder

6 large eggs
1 package Béarnaise Sauce Mix, prepared
   according to package directions

Preheat oven to 350 degrees. Cut each slice of bread into a 3-inch circle using a cutter or a glass. Press bread circles into 6 muffin tins that have been sprayed with nonstick cooking spray. Divide the bacon and green onions among the bread rounds, sprinkle each with a bit of garlic powder and top with an egg. Bake 20 minutes, until whites are set and yolks are soft but not runny. Remove from tins and top with the Béarnaise.

Makes 6 eggs.

Serve with: A fruit salad and some sweet muffins or coffee cake would make this a delicious way to entertain in the morning.

Quick Tip:

While I chose bacon and green onion as flavor boosters here, ham, cooked sausage or diced Canadian bacon all would be great. The green onions can be omitted, if desired. Some shredded cheese of almost any variety could be sprinkled on before or after the eggs are added.

Twice-Baked Potato Casserole

Cheesy Spinach Spaghetti

If you're looking for a change of pace from the usual spaghetti with tomato sauce, look no further than this recipe for Cheesy Spinach Spaghetti. This hearty casserole, a combination of cooked spaghetti, spinach, sour cream, milk, an egg and two kinds of cheese, is a real family pleaser. It's also a hit at covered dish dinners!

Cheesy Spinach Spaghetti

8 ounces spaghetti, cooked and drained
1 10-ounce package frozen chopped spinach
1 large egg, beaten
$1/2$ cup regular or reduced-fat sour cream
$1/4$ cup skim milk

4 tablespoons grated Parmesan cheese, divided
1 teaspoon onion salt
$1/4$ teaspoon freshly ground black pepper
2 cups shredded Monterey Jack cheese, divided

Preheat oven to 350 degrees. Cook spinach according to package directions, drain well and set aside.

Combine egg, sour cream, milk, 2 tablespoons of the Parmesan cheese, onion salt, pepper, spinach and 1 cup of the Monterrey Jack cheese in a large bowl. Add the spaghetti, tossing well to coat.

Pour the mixture in a baking dish that has been sprayed with nonstick cooking spray. Top with the remaining cheeses and bake for 30 minutes, until cheese is melted and top is lightly browned.

Makes 4 to 6 servings.

Serve with: Garlic bread and a fresh fruit salad. Orange or strawberry sherbet would be a nice, light dessert.

Twice-Baked Potato Casserole

I developed this recipe as a way to enjoy the flavors of my favorite twice-baked potatoes, while eliminating the steps of baking the potatoes, scooping out their pulp, combining the pulp with other ingredients and baking again. Serve with steak, a roast, or your favorite grilled entrée for a side dish your family will love!

4 cups prepared mashed potatoes*
2 tablespoons butter or margarine
$1/2$ cup chopped green onions
1 teaspoon garlic salt

$1/2$ teaspoon paprika
Dash cayenne pepper, optional
1 cup regular or reduced-fat sour cream
1 cup shredded regular or reduced-fat sharp cheddar cheese, divided

Preheat oven to 350 degrees.

Prepare potatoes according to package directions and place in a large bowl.

Melt the butter in a medium skillet over medium-high heat. Add the green onions and sauté until wilted. Pour over the potatoes. Add the garlic salt, paprika, cayenne, sour cream and $1/2$ cup of the shredded cheese. Stir well to blend ingredients. Taste for seasonings and add more

garlic salt or cayenne accordingly. Pour into a baking dish that has been sprayed with non-stick cooking spray. Sprinkle with the remaining cheese. Bake for 25 minutes, until cheese is melted and potatoes are heated through.

Makes 6 servings.

*Ore Ida frozen mashed potatoes, prepared according to package directions with skim milk, were used for testing purposes.

Spinach Oven Omelet

Spinach Oven Omelet

When I don't have a menu planned for dinner, often I turn to eggs. Whether scrambled, poached, fried or turned into an omelet, they quickly become the center-piece of an impromptu meal. With this spinach oven omelet, no sauté pan is required. The ingredients are simply stirred together in a bowl, poured into a baking dish and baked for 35 to 40 minutes.

4 large eggs, beaten
1 10-ounce package frozen chopped spinach,
   thawed and drained well*
1 16-ounce container reduced-fat cottage cheese
$^1/_4$ cup shredded Parmesan cheese

$^1/_2$ cup shredded Swiss cheese
$^1/_2$ teaspoon Beau Monde seasoning, optional
Dash Tabasco sauce
Dash ground nutmeg
Salt and freshly ground black pepper

Preheat oven to 350 degrees. Spray a 9-inch round bak-ing dish with nonstick cooking spray and set aside.

Combine eggs and spinach in a large bowl. Add cheeses and seasonings, mixing well. Pour into prepared dish and bake 35 to 40 minutes, until puffed and golden brown on top.

Makes 4 servings.

*Squeeze defrosted frozen chopped spinach with your hands or between two salad plates to remove as much liquid as possible.

Quick Tip:

While I use spinach and Swiss cheese as the main ingredients in this recipe, feel free to substitute your favorite vegetables or cheeses. Broccoli and cheddar are a nice combination, or use moz-zarella and defrosted pepper and onion stir-fry blend for a Mediterranean flavor.

Basil-Brie Pasta

Fresh basil is a backyard bonanza during the summer months. Sliced into a Chiffonade and sprinkled on fresh tomatoes, pureed into pesto or tossed into this Basil-Brie Pasta, I have no trouble finding ways to make use of this flavorful herb before the weather turns cool. This recipe is the perfect summer entrée, so keep it in mind for when the tomatoes are at their peak and the fresh basil is in abundance!

Basil-Brie Pasta

8 ounces spaghetti or other pasta
2 tablespoons olive oil
1 teaspoon garlic, minced (1 large clove)
1 cup (packed) fresh basil leaves, washed, dried and
 torn into small pieces

$^1/_2$ cup sundried tomatoes (not in oil), reconstituted
 according to package directions, if desired
8 ounces Brie, rind removed and cut into $^1/_2$ inch pieces
Salt and freshly ground black pepper, to taste

Cook pasta according to package directions. Drain and return to pan. Toss pasta with remaining ingredients and serve immediately. Season to taste with salt and pepper.

Makes 4 servings.

Serve with: This could be a one-dish meal, or you can serve with a fresh cucumber salad and crusty bread. Fresh peaches, peeled, cut into wedges and tossed with a bit of sugar, would make a wonderful dessert atop prepared shortcakes and vanilla ice cream.

Quick Tip:

While I suggest using Brie in this recipe, you could substitute Parmesan, or fresh mozzarella, which has recently become available in most supermarkets.

Another Quick Tip:

Cutting basil, spinach or Romaine lettuce into a chiffonade adds a flourish to your presentation. Simply stack washed and dried leaves on a cutting board, roll cigar-style and slice into thin strips.

Potato Casserole

Potato Casserole

Few recipes are as "multi-purpose" as this Potato Casserole. This is alway a hit as a side dish to grilled entrees or a holiday baked ham, a take-along to a covered dish meal or an addition to a breakfast or brunch buffet.

1 2-pound bag frozen Southern-style hash-brown potatoes, defrosted
2 cups regular or reduced-fat sour cream
1 10³/₄-ounce can regular or reduced-fat condensed cream of chicken soup
1 teaspoon salt
¹/₄ teaspoon freshly ground black pepper
2 cups shredded cheddar cheese
¹/₄ cup butter or margarine, melted
2 cups corn flakes, crushed

Preheat oven to 350 degrees.

Combine sour cream, cream of chicken soup, salt, pepper and cheese in a large bowl. Fold in the hash browns and pour into a 9-by-13 inch glass baking dish that has been sprayed with nonstick cooking spray. Combine the melted butter or margarine with the crushed corn flakes and sprinkle over top.

Bake for 45 minutes.

Makes 10 servings.

Sweet Potato Muffins

Muffin mixes are a convenient way to add to your menus, but you can whip up my homemade Sweet Potato Muffins in just about as little time. While many recipes calling for sweet potatoes require an hour of baking fresh sweet potatoes, time for cooling, then peeling and mashing, my recipe takes advantage of canned sweet potatoes. These muffins are a tasty alternative to blueberry or bran muffins on a breakfast buffet, but I find I serve them most often with dinner. Their sweetness is a nice contrast to a salad that's tossed with chunky blue cheese dressing, and they also pair well with a spicy bowl of chili.

¹/₂ cup butter, softened
1 cup sugar
2 eggs
1¹/₂ cups packed canned sweet potatoes, drained well and mashed
1¹/₂ cups all-purpose flour
2 teaspoons baking powder
¹/₄ teaspoon salt
1 teaspoon ground cinnamon
¹/₂ teaspoon ground nutmeg
1 cup skim milk
¹/₂ cup chopped pecans, optional

Preheat oven to 400 degrees. Spray muffin tins with nonstick spray and set aside.

Cream butter and sugar in a large bowl. Add eggs and sweet potatoes, and blend well. Combine the flour, baking soda, salt, cinnamon and nutmeg in a medium bowl. Add to the sweet potato mixture, alternating with the milk, until combined. Fold in nuts, if desired. Fill prepared muffin tins ³/₄ full and bake for 20 to 25 minutes for regular muffins, 15 minutes for mini muffins.

Makes 16 regular and 38 mini muffins.

Sweet Potato Muffins

Cheese Calzone

Cheese Calzone

This child-friendly recipe is the most basic of cheese calzones. Refrigerator pizza crust dough is wrapped around a filling of part-skim ricotta cheese, shredded mozzarella cheese, garlic salt and egg. While my cheesy filling is a real child-pleaser, feel free to stir in your favorite pizza toppings. Fresh sliced mushrooms, onion and bell pepper make a nice vegetarian filling, while browned sausage, cubed ham or pepperoni will satisfy your meat cravings.

1 10-ounce package refrigerated pizza crust dough
1 cup part-skim ricotta cheese
1 cup part-skim shredded mozzarella cheese
$1/_4$ teaspoon garlic salt
1 egg, beaten
1 egg white
Marinara, spaghetti or pizza sauce, heated, for dipping

Preheat oven to 400 degrees.

Remove pizza crust from the refrigerator and let sit at room temperature for 30 minutes.

Combine ricotta, mozzarella, garlic salt and egg in a medium bowl. Remove pizza crust dough from tube and cut into four equal portions. Roll each portion into a 6-inch circle on a well-floured work surface. Let sit 5 minutes, and then roll again, into 8-inch circles.

Divide the filling between the four circles, then brush the edges with the egg white and seal. Place on baking sheet and bake for 15 to 20 minutes, until crust is golden. Heat the marinara sauce and serve on the side.

Makes 4 servings.

Serve with: Raw baby carrots and ranch dressing. For dessert, pick up some fudge bars from the freezer section of your supermarket.

Quick Tip:

Allowing the dough to sit at room temperature for 30 minutes before opening the tube makes the dough easy to work with. I also recommend rolling each piece of dough into a 6-inch circle, then letting it rest a few minutes before rolling it out to the larger 8-inch circle called for. Both resting periods allow the gluten in the flour to relax, making rolling much easier.

Barb's Quick Tarragon Rolls

There's nothing like the smell of yeast rolls baking in the oven to get your family running to the kitchen. But with the kneading, rising and waiting involved, homemade yeast rolls are usually reserved for special occasions and holidays. At my house, homemade yeast rolls became a weeknight specialty when my neighbor, Barbara Mysona, shared her delicious recipe for Quick Tarragon Rolls. A speedy mix in a large bowl and a quick rise in muffin tins are all it takes to bring home-baked goodness to your table any time.

$2\frac{1}{2}$ cups all-purpose flour
1 teaspoon salt
1 package rapid rise yeast
1 tablespoon dried parsley flakes
1 teaspoon dried tarragon
1 teaspoon celery seed
2 tablespoons sugar
1 egg
2 tablespoons vegetable oil
1 cup warm water

Barb's Quick Tarragon Rolls

Preheat oven to 375 degrees.

Combine $1\frac{1}{2}$ cups flour with the remaining dry ingredients. Add the egg, oil and warm water and beat on low speed with an electric mixer for 30 seconds. Beat on high 3 minutes. Stir in remaining 1 cup of flour. Cover and let rise 15 minutes.

Spray muffin tins with nonstick spray and spoon in the batter, filling $\frac{1}{2}$ full. Let rise in a warm place until double, about 15 to 30 minutes.

Bake muffins for 10 to 12 minutes, until puffed and lightly browned on top. Remove from muffin tins and serve.

Makes 8 to 12 muffins.

Note: These rolls can be baked ahead, and freeze beautifully. Freeze them in zip-top plastic bags, then wrap in foil and reheat in a 350 degree oven for 10 minutes.

Quick Tip:

Using an ice cream scoop that has been sprayed with nonstick spray is an easy way to get sticky dough from the bowl and into the muffin tins.

Crockpot Scalloped Potatoes

Crockpot Scalloped Potatoes

My mother, Carol Gage, is famous for her cheesy scalloped potatoes. She combines peeled and sliced potatoes with a Mornay sauce (a white sauce to which shredded cheese is added), and then bakes the combination in the oven for an hour. I've toyed with the recipe, trying to come up with a version that's close to Mom's while eliminating several steps. This version is close, but for the real deal, you'll have to head south to Central Florida and visit my Mom.

Serve your Crockpot Scalloped Potatoes with steaks, chicken or pork chops hot from the grill. Or, you can turn this side dish into a simple and filling entrée by adding some diced smoked ham.

4 large baking potatoes, peeled and sliced
1 10 $^3/_4$-ounce can condensed cheddar cheese soup
1 10 $^3/_4$-ounce can condensed cream of potato soup
1 cup skim milk
1 teaspoon garlic or onion powder
Freshly ground black pepper, to taste
2 cups shredded regular or reduced-fat sharp cheddar
  cheese

Spray the inside of the slow cooker vessel with nonstick spray. Combine the soups, milk and garlic or onion powder in a medium bowl. Layer half of the potatoes on the bottom of the slow cooker. Sprinkle with pepper, spread with half of the soup mixture and sprinkle with half of the shredded cheese. Repeat with remaining ingredients. Cover and cook on low for 6 to 8 hours, or on high for 3 to 4 hours.

Makes 8 servings.

Cornbread Pudding

Corn pudding and cornbread are classic Southern dishes. When the two are combined into a hybrid recipe, you've got a side dish your family will love.

1 8.5-ounce box corn muffin mix*
1 16-ounce can whole kernel corn, drained
1 16-ounce can cream-style corn

1 stick ($^1/_2$ cup) butter or margarine, melted
1 cup sour cream
3 eggs

Preheat oven to 350 degrees. Combine all ingredients in a large bowl. Stir until well blended and pour into a 9-by-13-inch glass baking dish that has been sprayed with non-stick cooking spray. Bake for 45 to 50 minutes, until pudding is puffed and lightly browned around the edges.

Makes 10 servings.

*Jiffy Corn Muffin Mix was used for testing purposes.

Quick Tips:

Although the recipe calls for real sour cream and a whole stick of melted butter, decreasing the fat content to suit your family's diet is simple. Choose low fat or fat free sour cream, and substitute applesauce for the melted butter, for a version that's similar in taste and texture.

Have some fun with the recipe by adding extra ingredients. Shredded cheddar cheese, chopped red bell pepper or canned diced green chiles are all wonderful additions to the pudding.

Lite Stuffing

Lite Stuffing

On Thanksgiving, the turkey isn't the only thing that gets "stuffed." We humans do our share of stuffing ourselves on our national day of thanks. This recipe, from PHC Weight Loss Centers, weighs in at 110 calories and 1.8 grams of fat, a huge reduction in calories and fat when compared to the stuffing traditionally served at our table, with 304 calories and 17.4 grams of fat per serving.

1 loaf stale* reduced-calorie bread, cut into cubes
1 small onion, chopped
1 small green bell pepper, chopped, or 1 cup chopped celery
1 14.5-ounce can reduced-sodium chicken broth
$^{1}/_{4}$ cup chopped fresh parsley or 1 tablespoon dried parsley flakes
1 teaspoon poultry seasoning
1 teaspoon freshly ground black pepper
1 egg, beaten

Sauté the onions and green bell peppers or celery in a nonstick skillet that has been coated with nonstick cooking spray over medium-high heat until tender. Add a bit of the chicken broth if the vegetables begin to stick to the skillet. Remove from heat and cool slightly.

Place the bread cubes in a large bowl. Add the vegetables, seasonings and egg. Gently stir to combine. Drizzle with the remaining chicken broth and stir again.

Lightly pack the stuffing into the cavity of the turkey before roasting, or bake, tightly covered with foil, in a 9-by-13-inch glass baking dish at 350 degrees for 40 minutes.

Makes 10 servings.

*Place the slices of bread on wire cooling racks overnight.

Cinnamon Pecan Pull-Aparts

Carol Craig, my sous chef during the Masters and a talented artist and cook who taught china painting in Augusta for many years, shared this recipe with me when I was her student. I've seen many versions of the recipe, but Carol's is my favorite. The recipe takes advantage of the frozen yeast roll dough available in most supermarkets. The frozen "rocks" of dough are combined in a bundt pan with pecan halves, melted butter or margarine and a mixture of cook-and-serve vanilla pudding mix, white and brown sugar and cinnamon. Once assembled, the rolls get an overnight rise.

Butter, for greasing the bundt or tube pan
$^{3}/_{4}$ **cup pecan halves**
25 ounces frozen yeast roll dough, unthawed
$^{3}/_{4}$ **cup butter, melted (1$^{1}/_{2}$ sticks)**
1 3.5-ounce package cook-and-serve vanilla pudding mix (not instant)
$^{3}/_{4}$ **cup brown sugar**
$^{1}/_{3}$ **cup white sugar**
2 teaspoons cinnamon

Butter a bundt or tube pan well. Sprinkle pecan halves over the bottom of the pan. Place frozen rolls over pecans. Drizzle the butter over the rolls. Combine the vanilla pudding mix, sugars and cinnamon in a medium bowl and sprinkle over the rolls. Let rise overnight. (Do not cover, rolls will rise above the pan.)

In the morning, place pan in a preheated 350 degree oven and bake for 25 minutes. Invert onto a large platter and serve.

Makes 12 servings.

Cinnamon Pecan Pull-Aparts

Wilted Red Cabbage

Cabbage is often forgotten as a vegetable side dish, so bring it back to the table with my Wilted Red Cabbage. It's simple to prepare, and is a wonderful way to add this healthful vegetable to your menus! Serve alongside roasted pork, and save leftovers to make delicious pork and wilted cabbage sandwiches on toasted rye bread.

3 slices bacon
1 head red cabbage, rinsed, dried and cut into thin slices
3 tablespoons sugar
3 tablespoons cider vinegar
Salt and freshly ground black pepper, to taste

Cook the bacon until crisp in a large sauté pan or skillet. Remove the bacon, chop coarsely and set aside. Pour out all but 1 tablespoon of the bacon drippings. Return pan and heat on medium-high. Add the cabbage and sauté until slightly wilted, about 3 minutes, stirring often. Add the sugar and vinegar and sauté 3 to 5 minutes more. Season to taste with salt and pepper.

Makes 4 to 6 servings.

Wilted Red Cabbage

Two-Way Baked Rice

When Bond and I were first married we often shared weekend meals with Steve and Lisa Sheetz. Lisa made a quick Beefy Baked Rice dish that Bond really loved, and I made a similar Baked White Rice that Lisa enjoyed. Both are quick sides that cook up unattended in the oven.

Beefy Baked Rice
1 10³/₄-ounce can condensed beef consume
1 10³/₄-ounce can condensed French onion soup
1 stick (¹/₂ cup) butter or margarine, melted
1 cup long grain white rice

Preheat oven to 350 degrees.
Combine all ingredients in a baking dish, cover and bake for 1 hour.

Makes 4-6 servings.

Baked White Rice
1¹/₂ cups long grain white rice
3 cups reduced-sodium chicken broth
2 tablespoons butter or margarine
Dash salt, black pepper, cayenne pepper
  and garlic powder

Preheat oven to 350 degrees.
Combine all ingredients in a loaf pan.
Cover tightly with foil and bake for 1 hour.

8

Blueberry-Lemon Pound Cake

sweets&desserts

Blueberry-Lemon Pound Cake

I love using cake mixes to come up with simple desserts that taste like they're baked from scratch. And, over the years, I've come up with some tricks to make the best of convenient boxed cake mixes. My recipe for Blueberry-Lemon Pound Cake is the perfect example of the best of cake mix cooking, and is wonderful served as a simple, home-style dessert or an addition to a weekend brunch.

1 18.25-ounce Lemon cake mix
8 ounces cream cheese, softened
1 cup vegetable oil
3 eggs
1 teaspoon vanilla extract

$^1/_2$ teaspoon lemon extract
1 cup frozen blueberries
$^1/_2$ cup fresh lemon juice
2 cups powdered sugar
Additional powdered sugar, for garnish

Preheat oven to 350 degrees. Butter and flour a bundt pan, shaking out the excess, and set aside.

Combine cake mix, cream cheese, oil and eggs in a large bowl and beat with an electric mixer until fluffy, approximately 3 minutes. Stir in vanilla and lemon extracts and fold in the blueberries. Pour into the prepared pan and bake 1 hour, until a toothpick inserted in the center comes out clean.

Place the cake, still in the pan, on a cooling rack. Punch holes in the cake using a metal or bamboo skewer. Combine the lemon juice and powdered sugar and pour over the top. Cool cake completely in the pan. Invert cake onto a plate and dust with powdered sugar.

Makes 10 to 16 servings.

Butter Pecan Blondies

A buttery white brownie layered with melted caramel, chopped pecans and white chocolate morsels is a most appealing combination. With the help of a cake mix and a bag of caramels, these luscious holiday treats (or anytime treats) that can be whipped up in a snap.

1 14-ounce package caramels, unwrapped
1 5-ounce can evaporated milk, divided
1 18.25-ounce French Vanilla cake mix
$^1/_2$ cup butter, melted
1 cup white chocolate morsels
1 cup chopped pecans

Butter Pecan Blondies

Preheat oven 350 degrees. Place caramels and $^1/_3$ cup of the evaporated milk in a saucepan. Heat over medium-low, stirring occasionally, until caramels are melted, about 10 minutes.

Combine cake mix, melted butter and remaining $^1/_3$ cup evaporated milk in a large bowl. Press half of the cake mixture in the bottom of a 9-by-13-inch glass baking dish. Bake for 8 minutes. Remove from oven and sprinkle with the white chocolate morsels and the pecans. Drizzle with the melted caramel, and crumble the remaining cake mixture over the top. Return to oven and bake 18 to 20 minutes. Remove from oven and cool completely before cutting into squares.

Makes 24 small squares.

Buttermilk Pie

Buttermilk Pie

While Buttermilk Pie is a Southern tradition, its luscious, sweet-tart flavor should be a welcomed addition to summer picnics and parties anywhere. I began preparing Buttermilk Pie in college, before I was much of a cook. Like most custard pies, it's a cinch to put together. Bake it early in the day, or even a day before serving, then slice the pie and garnish with fresh berries for a Southern summer sweet.

1 unbaked refrigerated piecrust or frozen pie shell
1$\frac{1}{2}$ cups sugar
3 tablespoons all-purpose flour
3 eggs, beaten

2 tablespoons butter, melted
1$\frac{1}{2}$ cups buttermilk
1 tablespoon fresh lemon juice

Preheat oven to 350 degrees. If using a refrigerated piecrust, fit into a pie tin, trim and crimp edges and set aside.

Combine sugar and flour in a medium bowl. Add the eggs, butter, buttermilk and lemon juice and mix well.

Pour into the prepared pie shell. Bake 50 minutes to 1 hour, until pie is set. Remove from oven and cool on a rack for 30 minutes. Refrigerate several hours or overnight before serving.

Makes 6 to 8 servings.

Amaretto Chocolate Sauce

Amaretto Chocolate Sauce

Amaretto Chocolate Sauce is a great hostess gift during holiday party season, and can literally be whipped up in minutes. The Amaretto liqueur gives the chocolate a luscious almond flavor. If you'd rather not cook with alcohol, simply substitute 1 teaspoon almond extract for the Amaretto.
Serve warm over vanilla or coffee ice cream for a heavenly, quick dessert.

1 cup whipping cream
$\frac{1}{2}$ cup granulated sugar
6 ounces semisweet chocolate morsels

2 tablespoons butter
2 tablespoons Amaretto liqueur

Place cream, sugar, chocolate and butter in a double boiler over simmering water or in a medium saucepan. Simmer over low heat, stirring often, for 10 to 15 minutes, until chocolate and butter are melted.

Stir well, then whisk in the Amaretto. Serve warm, or refrigerate until ready to use. Reheat by placing in a double boiler over simmering water or in the microwave oven.

Makes approximately 2 cups of sauce.

Fudge Pound Cake

Fudge Pound Cake

Having a few good, quick desserts in your repertoire can be a coupe for busy cooks. That's why I always have a few hidden ingredients – cake and brownie mixes – stored away in my pantry. With a packaged mix as a base, you can whip up something that tastes practically "made-from-scratch," but with much less measuring! This Fudge Pound Cake is always a hit, and this recipe begins with a Devil's Food cake mix.

1 18.25-ounce Devil's Food cake mix
8 ounces cream cheese, softened
1 cup vegetable oil
3 eggs

$^{1}/_{2}$ cup chocolate syrup
1 teaspoon vanilla extract
1 tablespoon Kahlua or other coffee liqueur, optional
1 16-ounce tub prepared fudge frosting

Preheat oven to 350 degrees.

Butter and flour a 12-cup bundt or tube pan, shaking out the excess, and set aside.

Combine cake mix, cream cheese, oil, eggs and chocolate syrup in a large bowl and beat with an electric mixer until fluffy, approximately 3 minutes. Stir in vanilla and coffee liqueur, if desired, and pour into the prepared pan. Bake for 1 hour, until a toothpick inserted in the center comes out clean. Cool in the pan for 10 minutes, and then turn out onto a cooling rack.

Heat one cup of the prepared frosting in a small saucepan over simmer or in a microwave-safe bowl until it melts into a glossy glaze. (Reserve the remaining frosting for another use.) Drizzle glaze over cake.

Makes 10 to 16 servings.

Elizabeth's Moon Cakes

Elizabeth's Moon Cakes

Many families pass on heirlooms to their younger generations. From silver to artwork, these mementos from the past link one generation to another. While special "things" bring back memories of loved ones, it's the foods that were shared that are the true memory-makers to me. My Grandmother's "Moon Cakes" were served often at family gatherings, especially in the summer months. They're a wonderful not-too-sweet dessert that pairs well with ice cream or served alone, as a pickup dessert or with tea.

1 cup butter, softened (2 sticks)
1$^{1}/_{8}$ cups sugar, plus $^{1}/_{2}$ cup for topping
6 eggs
2 cups cake flour*

2 teaspoons baking powder
Grated rind from 1 lemon
1 cup finely chopped or ground walnuts or pecans

Preheat oven to 350 degrees.

Cream butter and 1$^{1}/_{8}$ cup of the sugar in the bowl of an electric mixture until fluffy. Add the eggs and beat again. Add the flour, baking powder and lemon rind and mix well. Pour into a greased half-sheet (11$^{1}/_{2}$-by-17$^{1}/_{2}$-inch) baking pan. Combine nuts and $^{1}/_{2}$ cup of sugar in a small bowl and sprinkle over the top. Bake for 15 to 20 minutes, until center is puffed and cake begins to pull away from the sides of the pan. Remove from oven and set aside on a rack to cool.

Cut the cake into crescents using a round biscuit cutter or juice glass. Begin in the left-hand corner of the baking sheet and cut a circle. Remove the circle to a rack. Next, use the cutter to slice a crescent-shaped moon from the edge left from the first cut. Continue cutting, beginning at the top of each row and working down. **

Makes 4 dozen crescents.

*All-purpose flour may be substituted for the cake flour.

**The cakes also may be cut into 2-inch squares.

Citrus Drops

Bridesmaid's luncheons, cocktail parties or large group gatherings all call for crowd-pleasing desserts in bite-sized servings. Lemon squares, brownies and cookies are all nice choices as pick-up desserts, but these Citrus Drops top them all in presentation and ease of preparation. This cake-mix recipe allows you to turn out 96 individual citrus cakes in under an hour!

1 18.25-ounce Orange Supreme or Lemon cake mix
1 3.4-ounce package lemon instant pudding mix
4 eggs
$^1/_2$ cup water
1 cup sour cream
1 16-ounce box powdered sugar
1 6-ounce can orange juice concentrate, thawed
3 tablespoons butter, melted

Citrus Drops

Preheat oven to 325 degrees. Spray two 24-cup miniature muffin tins with nonstick cooking spray. Place cake mix, instant pudding mix, eggs, water and sour cream in the bowl of a heavy duty stand mixer or large bowl. Beat with the stand mixer or an electric hand mixer on medium, until well blended and smooth. Spoon the batter into the prepared muffin tins and bake 10 to 12 minutes. Remove from oven and place on oven racks. Continue baking batches until all batter is used. You should have enough batter for 96 muffins.

While the muffins bake, combine the powdered sugar with the orange juice concentrate and melted butter. Beat until smooth using a hand whisk or electric mixer. As the batches of muffins come out of the oven, remove from the muffin pans and dip each muffin in the glaze by inserting a fork in the top of the muffin and dipping the bottom and sides in the glaze. Place on parchment-lined baking sheets, glaze side up, until glaze is set. These can be prepared several days before serving. Store in a container with a tight-fitting lid.

Makes 96 Citrus Drops.

Chocolate Chip Pie

I love participating in "group" meals — from our bimonthly supper club to church covered dish socials, it is great fun to bring a dish and sample the preparations of others. When I'm assigned a dessert, but have little time for something elaborate, I bake up a Chocolate Chip Pie. This crowd-pleaser comes together quickly, and doesn't need to be made ahead. Combine the ingredients, pour into a frozen piecrust and bake, and then tote to your destination. Warm slices of this pie are delicious topped with vanilla ice cream!

2 eggs
$^1/_2$ cup all-purpose flour
$^1/_2$ cup granulated sugar
$^1/_2$ cup brown sugar, packed
1 cup butter, melted and cooled (2 sticks)
1 tablespoon vanilla, Kahlua or bourbon
$^1/_2$ cup chopped pecans
1 cup semisweet chocolate morsels

Preheat oven to 325 degrees. Combine eggs, flour, sugars, melted butter and vanilla or other flavoring in a bowl and stir until well combined. Fold in chopped pecans and chocolate morsels, pour into pie shell and bake for 1 hour, until center is set.

Makes 6 to 8 servings.

Quick Cobbler

Quick Cobbler is the perfect ending to a lazy summer meal, and can be whipped up in a snap. I've had the recipe in my files for many years, as it was given to me at a kitchen bridal shower in which each guest brought a recipe. The original called for cherry pie filling, but I prefer a summer-inspired combination of peach pie filling and fresh blueberries. I've listed other delicious combination possibilities in my Quick Tips below. Whichever version you choose, all variations are even better topped with a scoop of vanilla ice cream.

2 21-ounce cans prepared peach pie filling
1 pint fresh blueberries, washed and dried
1 9-ounce "Jiffy" golden yellow cake mix*
$^1/_2$ cup butter or margarine, melted (1 stick)
$^1/_2$ cup chopped pecans

Quick Cobbler

Preheat oven to 350 degrees. Combine peaches and blueberries in a medium bowl and spread in the bottom of a baking dish that has been sprayed with nonstick cooking spray. Sprinkle the cake mix over the top and drizzle the butter over the cake mix. Sprinkle with the chopped pecans and bake for 40 to 50 minutes.

Makes 8 servings.

*One-half of a standard sized cake mix can be substituted for the Jiffy cake mix.

Quick Tips:

This recipe is a great beginning for other quick and easy desserts. You can use any pie filling that you like, and you can vary the flavor of cake mix, too.

Make Black Forrest cobbler by using cherry pie filling and chocolate cake mix. Apple pie filling and spice cake mix would be a tasty combination in autumn. Blueberry pie filling and lemon cake mix would be delicious. And, you could go tropical by using pineapple pie filling, yellow cake mix and a sprinkling of coconut with the chopped pecans.

Canadian Butter Tarts

Visiting Niagara Falls for the first time is awe-inspiring, to be sure. And, as a child, crossing from New York into Canada (my first foreign country) was a thrill. But perhaps the best memory from our family trip was the Canadian Butter Tarts we sampled at a roadside restaurant. A buttery pastry encased sugary sweet custard studded with raisins and walnuts. We definitely "couldn't eat just one!" When my grocer's freezer section carries packages of individual pastry shells, I head home to make the Butter Tarts. The recipe is a snap to prepare, and serving individual tarts for dessert makes them seem ever so special.

$^1/_4$ **cup butter, softened ($^1/_2$ stick)**
$^1/_2$ **cup brown sugar**
$^1/_2$ **cup light corn syrup**
2 eggs
1 teaspoon vanilla
$^1/_2$ **cup raisins**
$^1/_2$ **cup chopped walnuts**
1 8-ounce box frozen pastry shells
  (containing 8 shells)

Preheat oven to 325 degrees. Cream butter and brown sugar in a mixing bowl. Add corn syrup and eggs, stirring until well combined. Stir in the vanilla, raisins and walnuts.

Place pastry shells on a parchment paper-lined baking sheet. Divide custard among the 8 pastry shells. Bake for 35 minutes, until custard is set in the middle of each tart.

Makes 8 tarts.

Canadian Butter Tarts

Pecan Baby Cakes

I've been infatuated with the notion of "butter-pecan" desserts recently, and came up with another great dessert that highlights the flavor of my favorite ice cream. My Pecan Baby Cakes start with a cake mix, but end with rich, home baked flavor. Bake them up in individual cake tins, or in a half-sheet pan, then cut with a 3-inch round cookie cutter before serving. Top the warm cake with good vanilla ice cream and drizzle with my super-quick Butter Pecan Sauce for a memorable dessert.

1 18.25-ounce French   **1 cup white chocolate**
  vanilla cake mix   **morsels**
$^1/_2$ **cup butter (1 stick)**   **1 cup chopped pecans**
  melted and cooled slightly   **Vanilla ice cream**
1$^1/_3$ cups whipping cream   **Butter Pecan Sauce**
1 teaspoon vanilla extract   **(see below)**
3 eggs

Preheat oven to 350 degrees. Spray a half-sheet (11$^1/_2$-by-17 $^1/_2$-inch) baking pan* with nonstick cooking spray and line with parchment paper. Spray the parchment paper with the nonstick spray.

Combine cake mix, melted butter, whipping cream, vanilla and eggs in the bowl of an electric stand mixer or in a medium bowl beat on low until the ingredients are combined. Increase the mixer speed to medium and beat 2 to 3 minutes more. Fold in the morsels and pecans, spread in the prepared pan and bake for 20 to 25 minutes, until a pick inserted in the center comes out clean.

Serve warm, topped with vanilla ice cream and drizzled with the Butter Pecan Sauce.

Makes 10 to 12 servings.

*Cake batter can be baked in individual cake pans or cupcake tins. Simply spray the pans or tins with nonstick spray, fill $^3/_4$ full with batter and bake 15 to 20 minutes.

Butter Pecan Sauce:
1 cup caramel ice cream   **3 tablespoons whipping**
  topping   **cream**
$^1/_4$ **cup butter ($^1/_2$ stick)** $^1/_2$ **cup toasted chopped pecans**

Place all ingredients in a small saucepan and simmer over medium-low heat until butter is melted and sauce is heated through. Stir occasionally to combine the ingredients.

Makes 1$^1/_2$ cups of sauce.

Bond's Low Country Boil   *page 80*

INDEX

*Selecting fresh fruit at the supermarket is a fun
lesson for Karin's children, Tripp and C.C.*